Interventions is produced on the land of the Wurundjeri people of the Kulin Nation.

We acknowledge the Traditional Owners of country throughout Australia and recognise their continuing connection to land, waters and culture. We pay our respects to their Elders past, present and emerging. Their land was stolen, never ceded.

It always was and always will be Aboriginal land.

To my father, Ric Throssell
and to all those who have
similarly suffered from
the State's determination
to find them *guilty*
despite proven innocent.

First published 2021 by Interventions Inc

Interventions is a not-for-profit, independent, radical book publisher. For further information:
        www.interventions.org.au
        info@interventions.org.au
        PO Box 24132
        Melbourne VIC 3001

Design and layout by Viktoria Ivanova.
Photo of Ric Throssell on cover and in frontispiece by Gabriel Carpay, 1960s.
Poem 'Death of a blowfly' by Michael Dransfield, from Rodney Hall (ed): The second month of spring / Michael Dransfield, University of Queensland Press, St Lucia, 1980. Quoted in full with kind permission of University of Queensland Press.

Author: Karen Throssell

Title: The Crime of Not Knowing Your Crime: Ric Throssell Against ASIO
ISBN: 978-0-6487603-8-2: Paperback

© Karen Throssell 2021

The moral rights of the authors have been asserted.
All rights reserved. Except as permitted under the Australian Copyright Act 1968 (for example, a fair dealing for the purposes of study, research, criticism or review), no part of this book may be reproduced, stored in a retrieval system, communicated or transmitted in any form or by any means without prior written permission.

All inquiries should be made to the author.

 A catalogue record for this work is available from the National Library of Australia

Karen Throssell is an award-winning writer and poet, with five poetry collections and a book of creative non-fiction *The Pursuit Of Happiness* (1988). She has also published in journals and anthologies including *Overland, Westerly, Meanjin, Quadrant, Hecate* and *Artstreams*. Karen was shortlisted for the 2017 Book of the Year Award – Poetry (Society of Australian Women Writers) and an earlier version of *The Crime of Not Knowing Your Crime* was shortlisted in 2017 for the Dorothy Hewett award for works of creative non-fiction. Her work reflects her commitment to radical politics, literature and feminism.

Phillip Deery is a Cold War historian. His books include *Red Apple: Communism and McCarthyism in Cold War New York* (2014), *The Age of McCarthyism: A Brief History with Documents* (2017) and *Sparrows and Spies: ASIO and the Cold War in Australia, 1949-1975* (2022). He is an Emeritus Professor of History at Victoria University.

THE CRIME OF NOT KNOWING YOUR CRIME

RIC THROSSELL AGAINST ASIO

Karen Throssell

With a contextual essay
Venona, ASIO and Cold War Espionage
by Phil Deery

INTERVENTIONS
MELBOURNE

Death of a blowfly

For all dead 'suspects' and for all law dead

beat yourself to death
on this invisible

christ. it is
'shot while trying… '

you are etched on this
lacemaker's landscape
on the detective's boots
stitched by informers, whisperers

they grow rich on innocence
they didn't do it, not them

your eyes sewn closed
by a coroner, a sailmaker

they smile
look the other way

small men with knives

MICHAEL DRANSFIELD
THE SECOND MONTH OF SPRING

I have in front of me two photos of my dad, from different eras. One – the dad I remember best – in 1999, a year before he died at 76 from an overdose of the painkiller Doloxene. The other is a newspaper photo taken 50 years earlier, accompanied by sensational headlines about the Royal Commission into Espionage.

In the first photo, he is sitting beneath a portrait of his mother, Katharine Susannah Prichard, writer and founding member of the Australian Communist Party. Katharine's portrait is in many shades of brown pastel. She is wearing her favourite corduroy jacket; I remember it – quite radical clothing for a grandmother in the 1960s. She looks benign, calm, her grey hair in waves across her forehead, and she has a slightly sad smile.

Dad is staring, even glaring, at the camera. Maybe he was being interviewed by a journalist. He has a face that declares he does not suffer fools.

Ric, centre, and Dorothy Throssell and solicitor Dr Louat in 1955

This is my story – get it right.

He is hunched forward, hands clasped as if forcing them to be still.

How many times do I have to do this?

Tell these people, these snakes, these messengers of snakes,

who look like they're listening, nodding sympathetically, concerned,

'so unfair, gross miscarriage of justice' then slithering off

to their masters who twist and turn, leave things out, put things in,

so in the end it looks just like they want it, and nothing like the truth.

He is looking intensely at the camera, eyes boring in.

Listen to me will you? How can I make you hear me?

His mouth is set in a tight, almost sardonic line.

God, not again, and guess what will happen.

My father has written pages and pages: letters to papers, articles in journals, chapters in books, even a book, in an attempt to make them get the story straight, trying constantly to correct the misinformation.

After 50 years of it, he was tired but still determined.

The second photo appeared on the front page of both the *Herald Sun* and *The Australian* the day after the start of the Royal Commission into Espionage in Australia. He looks so very young, about 30, very good looking, dark hair with a cowlick on the side. People told him he looked like Gregory Peck. He is wearing a dark suit, white shirt and pale tie, and he is smiling (they said triumph; he said relief). Beside him is his beloved wife Dodie (Dorothy), whom Vladimir Petrov, the Russian spy who defected in 1954, also 'named'. She appears cool and beautiful, as usual, with her long hair and black beret. But he knows better, knows how traumatic the whole ordeal is for someone so painfully shy and reclusive, how offensive to her sense of justice is all the nonsense that is being hurled around.

In his own writing about the event, dad was first perplexed, then astonished, and finally appalled at what transpired. Some deranged Russian whom he had never met accused him of passing secrets.

What secrets? When? Where?

What madness it was.

There is an innocence in these photos. Dad was always an idealist, though not in the same way as his mother; he really believed in democracy – a fair go, a free and honest press, people innocent until proven guilty.

These men in the Royal Commission are Supreme Court judges.

They're there to find out the truth. Of course they will get to the bottom of it.

No one could possibly believe the evidence of this shambling Russian spy

who can't get his story straight and who clearly would say anything

to stay in Australia. They'll see straight through him.

Soon this nightmare will all be over.

ITEM #1

Facts about my father

(apologies to Lorna Crozier)

1.

He was six foot two.

He had black hair, dark brown eyes and pale Celtic skin that burned and peeled each scorching WA summer. In later summers, he had cancers lasered off his nose and shoulders.

2.

He had a good physique – broad shoulders and wide chest – and he took pride in it, doing sit-ups on the floor in his underpants every morning. When he was younger, chopping wood for our open fire was his major exercise, but he wasn't sorry to see it finally replaced by a gas 'Wonderheat'.

3.

Army mates of his dad's offered to pay for him 'to get a proper education' at Wesley, much to Katharine's consternation. Not only was it private, but it was religious! They eventually convinced her that it would afford a better education than the little local school and was too good an opportunity to miss… He apparently loved it and was even selected to be a prefect. He famously declined because he refused to swear on the bible.

4.

He wanted to be a film director, having a very early passion for theatre and film. Katharine was trying to send him to Moscow to study with Eisenstein (!) before war broke out. So he had to lower his sights and did a short stint as a trainee teacher before joining up.

5.

I recently spoke to an old bloke on his ninetieth birthday who had been a pupil at the school where dad worked at as a trainee teacher, and who remembered him. He said that the girls all loved him. He was so good looking, and he put on all these great plays.

6.

He even managed to produce a play during the war, in Milne Bay military hospital where he was recovering from malaria.

7.

He nearly died as a linesman in New Guinea – shot at by his own men. Apparently he was out in a row boat and they thought he was the enemy…

8.

Dad hated frangipani flowers. He said he couldn't see them on the ground without remembering the severed heads the Japanese left them to find – lying amidst the blossom.

9.

In the early years of my childhood, theatre was dad's passion. Weekends were learning lines and going to rehearsals at the little Canberra Repertory Theatre. On first nights, he would buy the women corsages of orchids. Afterwards, I'd get to meet them backstage, watching (rather aghast) at the transformation created by the removal of face paint and the peeling off of wigs. I can still smell that combination of make-up, cigarettes, alcohol and adrenaline.

10.

Some of his roles left a lasting impression: when he played the lead in his own play – *The Day Before Tomorrow* – he had very realistic 'burns' all over his shoulders and back, and he wouldn't remove them between the Friday and Saturday performances. So there he was, digging in the rose garden in his singlet with the skin hanging off his arms in shreds.

11.

He rarely got sick, believing that it was mostly in the mind. I only remember him once going to bed sick, and that was with hepatitis. He was very yellow. He also fell off a truck in the war, and the nerve damage turned into severe sciatica which plagued him throughout his later years. Not that he ever complained, but I found out how strong his painkillers were, and the extent of his pain, when he gave me one for a torn shoulder. It killed the pain dead and turned me into a zombie. He took 10 a day... They were called Doloxene.

12.

My sister tells me he had also had prostate cancer, which he kept so quiet, she only found out years later, and I only found out through her.

13.

Dad was a very convincing actor, and not just on the stage. Before Canberra got TV in the 1950s, we used to listen to radio plays on a Sunday night. There was a long-running science-fiction series where aliens would inhabit people's bodies – even the good guys, so you would never know who was friend or enemy. After it finished one night, dad came into the room with the very same slightly stiff walk and leaden voice as our alien humans. I remember screaming in terror because I was convinced he had been 'taken'.

14.

Some of the Wesley Methodist values rubbed off on him. He didn't believe in any kind of excess (except maybe on first nights) and had little interest in material possessions, being an early recycler and buyer of second-hand goods. The only time he spent a lot of money was on gifts. Then, he was generous to a fault.

15.

Both mum and dad were smokers, in the early days smoking with a holder, which I thought looked very arty. Dad often tried to give up, but he got so grumpy that we kids used to try to talk him into smoking again. He eventually taught himself self-hypnosis with the help of Dr Ainslie Meares. Then he was able to give up immediately.

16.

Dad was never interested in party politics, other than briefly catching the national euphoria when Gough Whitlam was swept into power. His main political passion was the peace movement, and in later years he became an active member of People for Nuclear Disarmament. He famously sold his father's VC to the RSL (who gave it to the War Memorial) and used the money to finance a film and a book called *The Pursuit of Happiness* about the need for nuclear disarmament.

17.

When I was young, we had occasional weekend outings which often involved collecting – mushrooms from the foothills around Canberra and oysters off the rocks at the South Coast. Mum and dad would take a bottle of sherry, two glasses, some lemons and an oyster knife. They would sit on the rocks and watch the sun set. I would lever the oysters off the rocks, and they would eat them. (I never liked them, but I loved 'catching' them.)

18.

Dad's favourite books were plays – Ibsen, Chekhov, Pinter, Beckett and then young Australians like David Williamson and Hannie Rayson. He only really started reading novels when he retired, though I do remember him reading *Cloudstreet* and not liking it. 'Too mystical,' he said.

19.

Dad claimed to be a feminist in terms of equality of opportunity and education, but was really of the old-fashioned 'protect and pamper' school. He shared much of the childrearing when time at the office allowed – but he apparently did the bulk of the midnight nappy changing and baby soothing, as well as making all our felt pilchers, when such things were worn. He also cooked dinner every Saturday night and did all the other washing up, until it became our job. He was a passionate exponent of the importance of a good education for all his kids, just assuming that we would all go to uni when we left school – an opportunity he had never had.

20.

He enjoyed good food and was an adventurous eater for his era, cooking things like curries and 'spag bol' and enjoying my attempts at elaborate French cooking. But his favourite breakfast was cornflakes with lots of sugar and the top of the milk. When he went through a health-conscious phase in the 70s, he switched begrudgingly to muesli and yoghurt. In his later years, he announced that life was too short to eat things you don't like, and went back to cornflakes, now with cream!

21.

Dad loved the bush, having spent his childhood in it, often on horseback. When I was young, we would all walk up Mt Ainslie, dad pointing out various wildflowers and shrubs by name. 'Learn from the bush,' he would say. 'Breathe it in... It can transport you, inspire you, heal you.'

ITEM #2

> The ethics of what had been done by unscrupulous journalism in a sickening echo of the Cold War witch-hunts remains to be dealt with by those whose role it is to protect professional ethics and the individual journalists who hope to preserve some respect for their profession.

They've done it again. A friend rang last night to tell me about another article in *The Australian* flogging the same tired old horse. Again.

The true facts are that initially and almost immediately, Venona identified nine spies, all members of the Communist Party of Australia (CPA) or closely aligned by family connections. Those spies were:

Walter Seddon Clayton, who was a senior CPA member and controller of the espionage ring.

Ric Throssell, external affairs officer, son of well known communist author Katharine Susannah Pritchard.

Dorothy Throssell, Ric's wife, also a member of the CPA and a member of the department of postwar reconstruction.

Katharine Susannah Pritchard, a member of the CPA and involved in transmitting to Clayton information obtained by her son Ric Throssell.

RETIRED ASIO OFFICER (ANONYMOUS)

I feel the familiar knot of anxiety in my stomach, the same slight wave of nausea, as I contemplate bringing it all back. Do I really want to whip myself into a frenzy typing up yet another furious response that will be ignored?

And if I don't, I will suffer all that guilt for letting them get away, yet again, with printing more deliberate misinformation.

I feel driven to defend dad against these continuing lies, but at what point does it become obsessive, carping? When do people's eyes glaze? When do they switch off at the mere mention of the topic?

I think of 'poor old Shirley Shackleton', who was trying to expose the cover-up of an international murder in Balibo, Indonesia, in 1976. Obsessive because her ex-husband was one of the victims. Finally, a filmmaker heard her and made *Balibo*, the film that forced the Indonesian government to admit that they had murdered five Australian journalists, including Greg Shackleton.

She finally got something like justice. No one says 'poor old Shirley Shackleton' now.

I go for a long walk around the gully to calm down. All full of the smell of spring – wafts of wattle, boronia and the odd bit of that evil escapee – pittosporum – still pervading the bush with its sweet perfume.

Dad was so passionate about the bush, always told me to soak it in, be more observant. He also said, you must always stand up for your beliefs, even when it is not what people want to hear.

And so I decide to have yet another go. Maybe someone will make a film about 'the man who had a mother'. I will keep exposing their lies as long as they keep writing them.

ITEM #3

Letter to the editor

(unpublished)

Submitted to *The Australian* 13 November 2010

Dear Sir,

In reference to your article of 13/11/2010 entitled 'The truth about our Russian spies,' does your anonymous author not know there was a Royal Commission into Espionage in 1955 which in fact completely cleared the Throssell family of the accusations of espionage dreamed up by the Russian Third Secretary Vladimir Petrov? Does your anonymous author not know that the Venona decrypts released in 1996 confirm that the Russians never had any interest in Ric Throssell or his mother, thus destroying the entire basis of the case against them?

Despite this and the fact there were never any charges laid against my family, Mr Anonymous still asserts 'they were spies.' So again, here are the facts:

The first part of Mr Anonymous's claim is correct. Katharine Susannah Prichard – my grandmother – was a communist, and Ric Throssell – her son and my father – did work in the Department of External Affairs. However, Ric never shared his mother's politics, describing himself in his book *My Father's Son* as a 'mild left-leaning Labor man.' The only 'organisation' he had ever belonged to was the Canberra Repertory Society.

My mother, Dorothy Throssell, was never a member of the CPA itself. As a philosophy student at Melbourne University, she belonged to the Eureka Youth League – the junior arm of the CPA. This was a period when the membership of the CPA was at its height, a time when it was almost mainstream for starry-eyed students to be fighting for the revolution. Dorothy let her membership lapse when she left university in the mid-1940s. She was a thinker, not an activist, and her 1945 diary clearly states that she was not impressed by the Soviet model from very early on in its history.

My grandmother, Katharine, was proud of being a founding member of the CPA. But of course, that does not make her a spy. In fact, she was an ardent nationalist (as expressed in almost all her novels), seeing little relevance to Australian society of the Soviet model of socialism.

Katharine was also fiercely proud of her son and respectful of his privacy and political independence. My father strongly asserts in his book that Katharine was never in the habit of discussing his career with other people:

> *We had the greatest confidence between each other with these limitations that she didn't discuss with me her political activities and I didn't discuss with her my official activities. I am sure she would not have discussed behind my back things that affected me personally.*

Yours sincerely

Karen Throssell

ITEM #4

Shirley Shackleton is my hero

How hard to keep going
with nobody listening
when to you it's so clear
and they don't want to know.

You're a thorn in their side –
What about Balibo?

A sad broken record –
Get over it, they say.
Famines, disasters, what can be done?
'Compassion fatigue.'

Tiny Timor, our wartime ally.
The brutal invasion – and we close our eyes.

'Poor Shirley Shackleton'
your eyes wide open
exposing war criminals
and defending the five.
Caught in the cross-fire – that's what they say.
We know it was murder.

Government cover-ups
no Assange, Snowdon, or Manning.
Even Gough turns away,
but Shirley persists.

Plugging away for twenty-odd years –
We watched them kill journos.

What about Balibo?
Oh it's just Shirley Shackleton.
Injustice fatigue, resistance fatigue,
or maybe the old She'll be right mate.

It is simply too hard.
They believed we would save them.

Shirley persists,
she takes them all on –
corrupt Indo generals and great Labor icons,
she keeps fighting until she has won.

ITEM #5

A man more sinned against than sinning

Dad loved Shakespeare. Like many people, he could quote most of the famous phrases; unlike most, he was intimately familiar with all of the plays – especially the tragedies.

As an actor, he played most of Shakespeare's tragic heroes, except Romeo and the British kings.

Macbeth stands out in my memory. Dad standing in front of the mirror practising his tortured look.

> Give sorrow words; the grief that does not speak knits up the o'er-wrought heart and bids it break.

Maybe this is because I still have on my walls both a large pastel portrait of dad as Macbeth and a handsome black-and-white photo of him in a fetching short tunic, with anguished face and drawn dagger. It was also the first performance I was allowed to attend in the little Canberra Repertory Theatre. And I was way too young. The only thing I remember is dad's head being brought out on a platter, blood dripping off the edge and onto the floor. *Daddy, Daddy!* I wailed in horror, while Mum bundled me out of the theatre, explanations that it was all papier-mâché and tomato sauce coming rather too late.

Over the years, the other characters I most remember are Othello (my black-faced father!):

> Reputation is an idle and most false imposition; oft got without merit and lost without deserving.

And my favourite, King Lear:

> I am a man more sinned against than sinning.

I have a wonderful photo of him in a moving open-book reading with my daughter Katie as Cordelia.

His was a heart-rending Lear. And not only his devoted family thought he was fantastic. Manning Clark, in a letter to *The Canberra Times*, stated that his interpretation of Lear would 'live for a long time in the minds of those who, like me, had the good fortune to see it.' On another occasion, he compared his performance to that of Olivier.

But it is Hamlet's most famous speech that dad uses tellingly in the foreword to his book, *My Father's Son*:

> To be, or not to be, that is the question:
> Whether 'tis nobler in the mind to suffer
> The slings and arrows of outrageous fortune,
> Or to take arms against a sea of troubles
> And by opposing end them.

ITEM #6

The Old King

(*vale* Ric Throssell 1922–99)

The old king has gone. Exit Stage Left.
Not to the thunderous applause for all those
Other exits, save that of jealous friends
Who wished to emulate his final Act,
Or cheered his greatness –
His late greatness.

He was the Prince of Denmark
Suffering slings and arrows,
Outrageous fortune, all his life.
But he did take arms against the world's
Troubled seas, personally feeling
All its pain, in his soul believing that
By opposing, he would help end them.
No more: no longer nobler in his mind to suffer,
To bear the whips and scorns of time.
He chose to die: a sleep to end
The heartache.

This Lear too,
Demanded extraordinary love
Of his beloved three – a love not even promised
By the snake-tongued sisters.
Sufficient love to let him go untimely.
And Lear raged with oak-cleaving thunderbolts
In a way our dear king did not.
He did not wish to live, pray, sing and tell
Old tales and laugh at gilded butterflies.
He chose to die: a sleep to end
The heartache.

Of the Scottish king, he shared no traits
Save his Celtic once-dark hair, and skin so fair
That carefree childhood under the wrong sun
Recalled a moth and flame…
And yes, he had ambition, no black and
Deep desires, but for an *end* to war.
His life a fight for peace, but too early
Thought his battle done, laid down his sword
And chose to die: Out, out brief candle
A sleep to end the heartache.
But hold, I cannot say Amen…

The old king is gone, our father, our king
And whilst he would have cried that
'Life's but a walking shadow, a poor player
That struts and frets his hour upon the stage,'
We too stood on that stage
Now empty, save for the heartache.

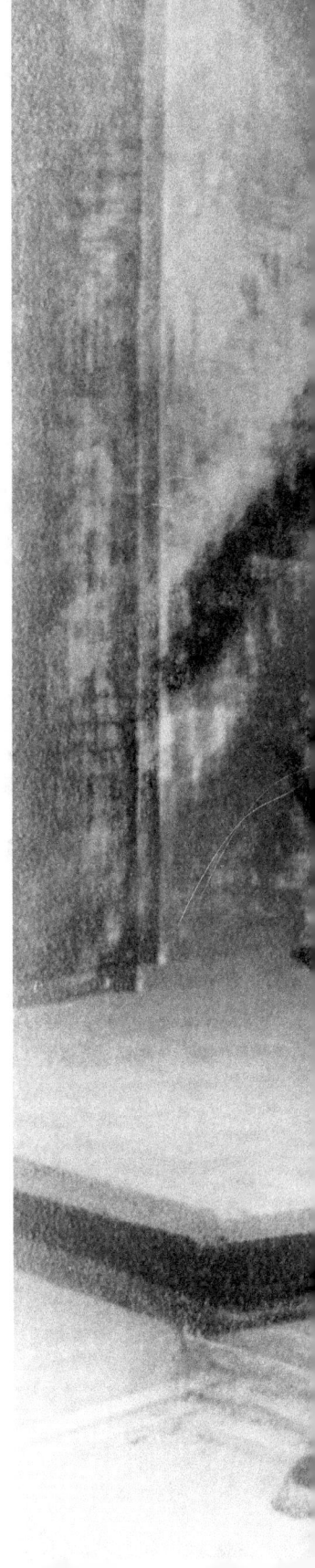

The Freedom of Information Act is adopted in 1982 and a year later extends the same principles of public access to secret historical documents in the Australian Archives when they are more than thirty years old (albeit with a huge range of exemptions).

With the friendly and efficient help of the Australian Archives staff I find the papers on KSP inherited by ASIO: and there among those papers from my secret past I discover the anonymous letter about the schoolboy son of that communist woman with which my file begins.

As I read, the image of another existence emerges. Observed, for all those years: schoolboy, student, soldier – I begin to see myself as they might have – those hidden men, those judging men.

The interest of the men in Moscow in those same indiscretions of my birth and position, has been seen as proof enough of disloyalty. I could trace the pursuit. It is hard to believe it could happen here. I drive home from the archives feeling as if I had seen a glimpse of myself in a twisted window. Sick of the unfairness of it, I know that there is nothing I can do now to tell them how wrong they have been. Those diligent men do not want to know. It has always been like that.

Turn and they are gone.

ITEM #7

The man who had a mother (1)

In the name of this theory

That we all hold so dear

You blacken the life

Of an innocent man

Not even a stirrer

He just had a mother

In this best of all worlds

With its truth

And its justice

See what you've wrought

On the life of this man

Who just had a mother

The law of the land says

Guilt must be proven

All this man's charges

Thrown out by the courts

But that's not enough

The man had a mother

And throughout the years
You still hiss your slander
Ignoring the courts
And laughing at truth
What does it matter?
The man had a mother

The slow poison lingers
Mustard gas, napalm
Those stuck in the Cold
War doing their best
Destroying the peace
Of the man with the mother

ITEM #8

insinuate

v. 1. suggest or hint (something bad) in an indirect and unpleasant way 2. (insinuate oneself into) manoeuvre oneself gradually into (a favourable position) insinuation n. an unpleasant hint or suggestion

ITEM #9

The Red witch of the West

(well of course she was...)

She lives alone in a wild green tangle –
a magic glade growing
in moon-washed night

> She lives *alone!*
> Who knows what she grows?
> Digitalis, wolf-bane, devil's-claw...

She has a pet magpie, named Caruso
He sings in kookaburra, currawong
sometimes chainsaw

> Of course, her familiar!
> She *talks* to him, he answers
> Who knows what else they get up to?

There is brewing:
dreams and tomorrows
wild women with books

                        Mad midnight dancing, probably naked
                            We know what those books were –
                                   Grimoires and Shadows

Like other bohemians, defying convention,
she smokes (with a holder)
wears black velvet pants

                                    An old woman in trousers!
                                    There was probably a cloak
                                    And look! There's the broom!

They did have their chants – *Workers Unite!*
not very different from
Never hunger, Never thirst

                                          So there you are
                                      Confess or you'll burn!
                              And remember, we have your son…

ITEM #10

My Fairy Godmother

(for KSP)

She made me a set of Cinderella dolls
although she said she couldn't sew. Cinderella,
her two sisters, who weren't all that ugly
and the Fairy Godmother.

As big as your hand, they had long velvet skirts
soft silky velvet, the real sort
with brocade bodices, lawn petticoats
and tiny lace knickers.

Such love sewn into their whimsical faces
and into each strand of fine woollen hair.
A Prince Charming too, but he's long disappeared,
if he ever really was there.

Best of all was the Fairy Godmother.
She wore a short black skirt, revealing
 long black legs, a great big smile,
and a red pointed hat.

I *loved* her, and I don't ever remember wondering
where the gauzy dress and the wings were.
Maybe I just always knew that godmothers
were more likely to be witches.

This small collection sums my gran up.
They are her hard and soft –
the soft velvet and the strong message,
the deep thought behind all she did.

The doting gran and the wild bohemian
who wore trousers and smoked
when it was definitely Not Done.
the stern ideologue with a photo of Stalin

Lived alone in the hills,
entertained Russian sailors,
had a pet magpie
who sang for his steak.

She definitely wasn't your typical gran
Spent her time writing
and changing the world
until the only child of her only child

arrived and was showered with love
and politics and told proudly
that her gran was called
'the Red Witch of the West.'

As I line them up now
faces faded, arms missing, very little hair,
except for our godmother who had none at all
just her red hat.

I see for the first time, that under her skirt
there's no lawn or lace
but bright red knickers.
Like a message in a bottle.

ITEM #11

My Fairy Godmother

Katharine is basically self-educated. In a world where families (including hers) could only afford to educate the boys, to keep pace with her friends who went to university, she:

> borrowed all the books they were reading from the public library: bought the penny classics and the second-hand editions of the great works of literature and philosophy and went on to devour the masterpieces of the French and German languages.

My grandmother becomes a journalist, like her father before her. In 1908, she travels to London to cover the Franco–British Exhibition for *The Herald*. This is almost unheard of for a woman at this time.

This is to be the beginning of her practical political education.

Katharine is already a very compassionate person; while living with wealthy relatives on their grand estate in the country, she is shocked and subsequently radicalised when they turn away starving men begging at the gate.

She decides then to move out and live 'like the real people.' Katharine is saddened, horrified, then angry about the huge inequalities she finds in London. From there, she begins reading all she can about theories on how to make society more just – finally deciding that Karl Marx and his 'scientific socialism' is the answer.

Once converted, my grandmother becomes a dedicated and unswerving founding member, party worker, public speaker and pamphleteer for the Australian Communist Party. Like most Marxists at the time, she believed that the essential battle was about class; to fight for disparate groups within that division (e.g. women, Aboriginal people, people with disabilities) was to fracture the cause. A society of equals means equality of the sexes. Everyone would benefit, come the revolution!

But Katharine is no mere ideologue. She lives her beliefs. I am brought up with the dictum that she teaches my father: *From each according to their abilities, to each according to their needs.* On the tiny earnings from her war widow's pension and her writing, she is generous to a fault. If a friend admires something of hers, she immediately gives it to them. If her wily granddaughter asks for a 'bride doll', she finds some way to get one for her. She once spends an entire royalty cheque on a set of teeth for the old bloke who occasionally helps in her garden. And it is mainly gifts that are bought for her that she gives away. She rarely, if ever, buys anything for herself.

I am very hurt when she gives away the little red Finnish teapot that I saved up and bought for her. I tell her that people usually only admire things to be polite. It doesn't mean they actually want to have them…

She disapproves of television, seeing it as a great time waster. There are never enough hours to read all the great books, if you ever have spare time for such indulgences. Most of her life is divided between Party work and writing. She has great discipline, rising early each morning and going down to her shack in the bush to write for about six hours a day.

My grandmother adores her little family, writing to dad and, later, to me every week, and giving us a wonderful welcome whenever we are able to make the long trek by car across the Nullarbor. She is always delighted when we arrive, doing a little dance of joy at the gate when she finally sees our trusty Hillman bumping up the dirt track. She always makes us each a pot of our own special jam: cape gooseberry for mum, strawberry for me, and fig for dad.

In her autobiography, *Child of the Hurricane*, Katharine describes one of the most momentous years of her life, 1933:

> [M]y sister, who was making a trip abroad, begged me to join her and be her guide in Paris. She sent the fare and Jim [her husband Hugo] insisted that I should take advantage of it to meet my English and American publishers in London, and perhaps go on to the Soviet Union. 'I'll never forgive you,' he said, 'if you don't try to see what's happening there. We must know whether what we've been told is true.'

So Katharine visits Russia, but while she is there, her beloved husband Jim, desperate and worn down by the Depression, kills himself. She is on a London bus, just before leaving for home, when she sees a billboard screaming AUSSIE VC SUICIDES.

When Katharine dies in 1966, she bequeaths her Russian royalties to me. I can only claim them by collecting them on Russian soil. In my early twenties, as part of the obligatory Aussie OS trek, I visit Moscow to collect my roubles and to see for myself.

ITEM # 12

Postcards from Russia

My darling Jim and little Nicky,
It is extraordinary here!
Roaming about in my wilful way
Nobody telling me where to go
I feel like a motherless foal
Dazzled and bewitched
By the power and beauty of it all

                                         Your Katharine (1933)

Dear Mum and Dad,
Moscow – drive from the airport
Snow covered pine forests
Hunkering down
Baba Yaga houses teetering
On hens' feet
I expect to hear sleigh bells

                                         Lots of love, Karen (1970)

My darling loves,
Moscow – sparkling new city
She looks like an aged courtesan
Beloved by a sturdy worker
New vitality permeating medieval veins
Red walls, white palaces
Gilded domes mirrored in the river

                                         Your Katharine (1933)

Dear Mum and Dad
Workers at the Bolshoi
Still in overalls and cloth caps
Arms full of roses to throw to the primas
Imagine seeing that at home!
                    Lots of love Karen (1970)

My two wonderful boys,
Organisation – the vital word
In the Stalin Auto plant
The ball-bearing factory
The Voroshilovka Mine
Organisation is father mother
Brother sister to them all
                    Your Katharine (1933)

Dear Mum and Dad,
Workers' palaces in the metros
Paintings on walls, shivering chandeliers
A small glimpse at the lives of the rich
As workers rush home from factories and mines
I wonder do they appreciate the gesture?
                    Lots of love Karen (1970)

My darling Jim, and Rikky-Tikky-Tarvy
My big trek to Siberia
The happiest folk I have met
Collective farmers
Rejoicing after a record harvest
The new season's sowing
Ploughing back in
                    Your Katharine (1933)

Dear Mum and Dad
Book stalls on the streets
Nothing but classics, mostly Russian
Tolstoy, Chekhov, Pushkin
But Shakespeare was there too and Dickens
Devoured just like Footy Times
And form guides back home

        Lots of love Karen (1970)

My darling Jim and Ric,
Feathers of snow
Soft kisses on lashes
Blurring the outlines
Of the Voroshilovka Mine
Standing stark
Against dark Siberian hills

        Your Katharine (1933)

Dear Mum and Dad,
So cold here
I wish I'd listened –
Packed the prickly long-johns
So cold that my slightly exposed chin
FROZE on a one block walk
To the Bolshoi
Lock-Jaw!

        Lots of love Karen (1970)

My dearest loves,
To see socialism happening!
Everywhere the Soviet government
Creating order
Out of the chaos of centuries
Truly inspiring
We now know it can be done!

       Your Katharine (1933)

Dear Mum and Dad
At home everyone told me
They'd want to buy my jeans here
So I learned how to say
'Ya Avstralitskya Comsomolskya'
Meaning Go away I support the system
No one has approached me yet
                              Lots of love Karen (1970)

Dearest Jim and little Ric
I thought you'd like to know I'm eating well!
Breakfast at the stolovyah
Meat rissoles, blenchki with thick Siberian honey.
But I do miss your porridge my love
And breakfast all together...
                              Your Katharine (1933)

Dear Mum and Dad
I can't take to hard rye bread
And salami for breakfast
Long for vegemite toast
Give me a beer over vodkha
But I love the bourscht
And they have the best ice-cream!
                              Lots of love Karen (1970)

Dearest Jim and little Nick
Last few days and I'll soon be home
Soviet officials ask me
Not to paint too rosy a picture. 'We communists are realists,
We are not yet a workers' paradise
And we have nothing to fear from criticism.'
                              Your Katharine (1933)

Dear Mum and Dad
Finally got my roubles!
How odd that inheritance is allowed
Surely 'unearned gains'
But I am told I must help the economy
Spend it here
So — vodka, fur hats and a silver samovar!
                              Lots of love Karen (1970)

Dearest Jim and Ric,
So there you are my precious loves
So little to criticise really
Such wonderful lessons
But it is still not home
And there is still not you
Whom I so long to see
                              Your Katharine (1933)

ITEM #13

The man and his mother

Dad was famously very close to his mother – so close that, according to ASIO, you couldn't distinguish between them.

The whole family would trek over the Nullarbor to see her, putting the car on the train at Kalgoorlie. As a student, I flew over by myself every year till her death, once becoming her 'secretary' and typing responses to her fan mail on the little Olivetti she gave me, which I still have.

They wrote to one another every week, and dad visited by himself at least once a year – more often as she got older and plane travel more accessible.

For dad, their regular communication was never a duty. They adored one another, though not uncritically; they debated many issues quite fiercely. Apparently, childrearing was one. Like many others at the time, my parents were seduced by the stern regimes of the Kiwi child-rearing 'expert', Sir Frederic Truby King. He believed in discipline and detachment – strictly 10 minutes a day for 'cuddles'. Katharine, who was more of a Dr Spock style of grandmother (the more cuddles the better), was horrified and attempted to subvert the regime. Without her intervention, who knows how I would have turned out.

Dad and Katharine were always discussing literature, social issues and politics, but they both had a deep respect for each other's different views, knowing that they each had their own way of fighting for the underdog and living a meaningful life.

There were times when we had disagreed, but never with the kind of disillusionment that could destroy respect and love between those more deeply devoted to the encompassing ideals of the communist revolution than I was. I was disturbed to see 'Uncle Joe – the wise and understanding leader of the Soviet people' whom Katharine had described to me as a boy, transformed into Generalissimo Stalin, the infallible military genius of the USSR, whose every retreat was a cunningly planned stratagem and each victory a personal triumph, his austere olive drab tunic changed into a General's uniform heavy with braided epaulettes adorned with all of the honours and medals of the Soviet State, praise to his name and title the obligatory preamble to every official announcement. What had happened to equality and brotherhood I asked?

When I first started studying politics at university and announced to Katharine that I didn't like this idea of the collective – *I was an individualist* – she listened attentively to my half-baked views and then spoke a bit about individuals within the collective. Never once did I feel that she was belittling my views or preaching. It was quite unusual for someone with her strength of conviction.

And with dad and his 'little mum', there was also that protective element. He was of that generation, and there she was, defiantly alone in the fire-prone Perth hills. Though she always resisted, dad was forever thinking of ways to make her life easier – a much-loved record player; a new fridge; and, after a fight, a modern hot water service to replace the old chip heater.

Katharine died of a stroke at 86, when dad was on his way to visit her. He arrived to find an ambulance in the driveway instead of her waiting at the gate. He never got to say goodbye. While he wore his heart on his sleeve in many ways, he was of the stoic, stiff-upper-lip school when it came to grieving. After the funeral, where the coffin was draped in a red flag, and the conservative Throssell clan were handed the words of *The Internationale* to sing, he buried his heartache. He rarely spoke of her death. He kept his grief tucked tightly inside, but it pulled long lines onto his face and hollowed his eyes for years.

The man who had a mother (2)

Had a Dad too, for a while

often at home in the growing years

taught him the joy of a ride

through the bush

sat him on a horse

when he was a chubby cheeked two year old!

Taught him to box on the grape festooned verandah

some quick wisdom thrown in:

if a thing's worth doing it's worth doing well

Always work on a face

Crack hardy like a Light Horseman

Don't let the sun set on your anger

Then his mum went to Russia
his Dad sad and strange
died suddenly and his mum didn't
even get to say goodbye…
She came home sad and strange
Then they were just two …
clinging together, hugging away their loss

Less time in her writing shack
she poured all that precious Jim love
into her only child
who had to become 'the man of the house'
carting firewood, feeding chooks
cooking the morning oats with raisins and honey
Until a soldier mate of his Dad's
paid for boarding school…

But those 'just-us-two' years
those desolate years
where the boy understands even then
her sacrifices made. That time helped
 put the pieces together, helped them hang on
cemented them forever
That man had a Mother

*

His granddaughter too
had a short-term Dad
much shorter term
though she did get to know him
when she was grown

She too had her single mum
bonded more by hardship, than grief,
not the apples and porridge kind of hardship
but a full-time job, and a two-person mortgage,
loneliness, and gold-plated child care
Not just double the work and the pain
but double the joy and the love

The granddaughter now
has a long-term bloke, kids of her own
Remembers those 'just-us-two' years
those desolate years of doing without
understands the sacrifices…
how much that time helped
put the pieces together, helped them hang on
cemented them forever
That girl had a Mother

ITEM #14

idealism

n. 1. the practice of forming or pursuing ideals, especially unrealistically. 2. (in art or literature) the representation of things in ideal form. 3. *Philosophy* any of various systems of thought in which the objects of knowledge are held to be in some way dependent on the activity of mind.

ITEM #15

Atheism

One strong view dad might have inherited from his mother was his atheism. But, of course, one could argue that scepticism about the supernatural reflects intelligence rather than genes.

Like his mum, dad was not a 'wishy washy agnostic.' He was quite certain there was no god.

> We laughed at the Romans who had lots of them for different things – war, love, travel, money, having a good time. Why is one who covers all bases any more believable?

He used to delight in questioning the earnest young Mormons proffering their Book, 'proving' Jesus actually started his preaching in the US. Dad would invite them in for a cup of tea, much to Mum's chagrin. She was a philosopher: there was no possible benefit in debating the ridiculous with the beguiled. He would then produce *his* books – the *Iliad* and the *Odyssey* – and say, 'Well, my books say this...' The confused and tongue-tied young men would let their tea grow cold and flee.

I wasn't allowed to attend scripture at school, unless I went to a different one each week. For a while, I sat in the playground with a couple of Jewish kids and the one exotic Sikh, but then I got bored and thought I'd try to do it dad's way. Of course it worked. They all told such different stories, were so clearly touting their wares and bagging the other lot, that I gave up and ended up wagging school on scripture morning.

But I did really want to go to Sunday school, which I was also forbidden to do until I was old enough to make up my own mind (dad muttering about Jesuits and *give me a child until the age of seven...*).

But they seemed to have fun. Sunday school picnics, lovely little cards you stuck into special books... I wanted at least to try it. I was a very determined and rather devious kid, so I organised to have a sleepover with a church-going friend on a Saturday night, just to experience the wonders of Sunday school for myself.

I should have taken note of the 'school' bit in the title. In fact, it was incredibly tedious – like the worst of school, without the interesting stuff. You didn't get the little cards unless you knew your silly words, and I decided that the picnics must have been a con to hook you in. The rest was just chanting and tests on how much of the bible you knew. I talked to dad about it years later, when older daughters could confess their sins, and he admitted that he had been wrong to ban it. He should have given me credit for working it out for myself.

ITEM #16

In 1943, the US Army Signal Intelligence Service began intercepting, then decrypting, cable traffic between the KGB and its officers around the world. This was a top-secret operation, code-named Venona, which eventually lead to the formation of ASIO in 1949.

Venona operated for 37 years. It revealed extensive Soviet espionage networks in the West including the Manhattan project at Los Alamos, which produced the atomic bomb in 1945. It also exposed names such as the Cambridge spy ring, and Julius and Ethel Rosenberg. The information remained secret for 15 years and much of it was only declassified and released in 1995.

The Venona decrypts confirmed that Katharine Susannah Pritchard had discussed with Clayton how Ric's career might be of use to the Soviets.

ASIO inferred from this that Katharine had actually influenced his posting to Moscow, and they therefore assumed that, once there, he would naturally be of use to Moscow.

ITEM #17

Peter Heydon (Senior officer of the Department of External Affairs in charge of administration and postings) had thoughts about Ric's posting:

> Throssell's a radical, so... let's post him to Moscow, let's see how he reacts to Russia on the ground. It will probably do him a great deal of good... Peter Heydon thought that exposure to the Russian system would cause him to drop the stars out of his eyes.

ITEM #18

Wonder and excitement

(Ric in Russia)

Dad was 23 when he was posted to Moscow as Third Secretary to the Australian Legation. He had just married his sweetheart, Bea, and she was to follow when she could get passage by sea. He writes like an excited kid on his first big outing. Well, it was, if you don't include Milne Bay during the war. Full of wonder and excitement at the strangeness of it all.

> Night began at three in the afternoon during the Moscow winter. The sky was a grey blanket over the city. Snow piled high in the side streets. The lights were on all day in the office. Nightfall came almost un-noticed.
>
> We saw block after block of solid suburban establishments, the monuments to socialist construction in concrete, among the surviving buildings of the old regime, squat thick walls in pink and yellow whitewash, the heroic statues of triumphant workers holding aloft the hammer and sickle, the benevolent smiling photos of Stalin, incomprehensible graphs of production figures. Quite enough for a start...

His stories were quite unlike Katharine's glowing praise for all the 'evidence' she found of socialism working. No hint of irony in her accounts.

Dad's account of what was basically his first adult job (after his brief stint as a relief teacher before the war) was full of the same boyish wonder:

> To me it was an exciting new world. Top Secret messages sounded important, even if they did not seem so momentous when the text emerged from the jumble of meaningless numbers. I was always sure that we had got it wrong, but even when my laboured efforts went astray, Mac managed to make sense of it.

The spycatchers saw it as 'alarming' and then later as 'evidence' that he was working in Moscow deciphering codes – a job that the Department of External Affairs had appointed him to. It seems highly unlikely that he would have included this breathless and somewhat naive description of his work in his autobiography if he was then leaking the information to the KGB.

His time in Moscow was also the time when, after only several months of married life, Bea was to contract the little-known disease, polyneuritis, and die very suddenly. Ric returned home, grief-stricken, within a year. Could he possibly have been 'accepting approaches' from the KGB at this time?

> I agreed to stay on for a short while in Moscow. The Chargé d'Affaires was needed at the Paris Peace Conference. Perhaps the responsibility of being in charge at the Legation would ease the emptiness of knowing that she was not there. But nothing seemed to have meaning for me. There were letters from my mother, broken, grief-stricken messages full of loving comfort. I longed for home.

ITEM #19

In mid-1952, Ron Richards (from ASIO) sought an interview with Throssell.

> As a result of the interview Colonel Spry [head of ASIO] wrote to the Minister for External Affairs informing him that Throssell had been assessed as 'not constituting a security risk to the Commonwealth.' Spry's letter…seems to make clear that **nothing in the deciphered MVD traffic, which had implicated Ian Milner and Jim Hill, implicated Ric Throssell**.
>
> There the question of Throssell rested – until the defection of the Petrovs.

ROBERT MANNE

I wade through the sorry record year by year and always somewhere beyond is the unspoken story, the unrevealed report, the undisclosed source, the 'evidence' that cannot be questioned cannot be seen.

ROYAL COMMISSION ON ESPIONAGE 1955

COMMONWEALTH OF AUSTRALIA

(Copyright in this Transcript is the property of the Crown. The Transcript may be copied only with the prior approval of the Attorney-General of the Commonwealth.)

ROYAL COMMISSION ON ESPIONAGE

OFFICIAL TRANSCRIPT OF PROCEEDINGS

TAKEN AT

SYDNEY ON TUESDAY, 1st FEBRUARY 1955

(Ninety-second Day)

(Continued from 27th January 1955)

(Note.—The proceedings on 28th January were held in camera, and the record thereof does not appear in this Transcript.)

PROCEEDINGS	Page
1. Statements by Dr. Louat, Q.C.	1977-9
2. Statements by Mr. Windeyer, Q.C.	1978
3. Evidence by V. M. Petrov	1979-96
4. Tendering of Exhibits 380 and 381	1995
5. Tendering of Exhibit 382	1996
6. Evidence by E. A. Petrov	1996-7

Royal Commissioners—
THE HONOURABLE MR. JUSTICE OWEN
THE HONOURABLE MR. JUSTICE PHILP
THE HONOURABLE MR. JUSTICE LIGERTWOOD

Secretary—
Mr. K. H. HERDE

Interpreter—
Mr. A. H. BIRSE

Mr. W. J. V. WINDEYER, Q.C., with him Mr. G. A. PAPE and Mr. B. B. RILEY, appeared to assist the Commission.
Dr. F. LOUAT, Q.C., with him Mr. S. G. CORY, appeared, by leave, for Ric Prichard Throssell.

RIC PRICHARD THROSSELL, sworn:

590. MR. WINDEYER.—What is your full name, please?—Ric Prichard Throssell.

591. Your name is not Richard, but just Ric?—Yes.

592. You are an officer in the Department of External Affairs?—Yes.

593. What is your present address?—My home address is 44 Ebden street, Ainslie.

594. I notice that you took an oath. I take it that you regard yourself as bound by your oath?—Yes.

595. You have said on occasions—and I am asking this only because you have done so—that you are an atheist?—No, I do not think that is right.

596. You have not said that?—No.

597. You made no such statement?—I have said I am an agnostic.

598. At all events, though you are an agnostic, you regard yourself as bound by your oath?—Yes.

599. You were seen by Mr. Richards on the 22nd July of last year, were you not?—Yes.

600. Did you say to him that you thought the interview must be in connexion with the Royal Commission?—I do not remember the form of words used, but I may have said something to that effect.

601. Did you say to him that you thought that your name might be on some list?—Yes.

602. Why did you think your name might be on some list?—I had been interviewed by the Security people some time before and, as I understood, cleared of any

612. PHILP, J.—That is, in 1953?—Yes.

613. MR. WINDEYER.—Yet when you read the proceedings of the Petrov Commission you felt that your name might be on a list?—It would not have surprised me if it had been.

614. It would not have surprised you?—No, because it was suggested to me that I would be such a person.

615. You were present in the court-room, I think, while Mr. Petrov gave his evidence?—Yes.

616. Assuming that what he said as to the contents of the cable is true, can you suggest any reason why you should be referred to in a cable from the Soviet in that way?—I can only suggest that the Soviet must have been misinformed by some person as to my standing.

617. Did you ever give any information to any Communist person which you, looking back on it, think any Soviet official might regard as valuable?—As far as I know, I have never given any classified information to any unauthorized person at all.

618. But I was asking you whether, looking back on it now - - -?—Yes.

619. - - - you think you ever gave any information to any Communist person which a Soviet official might consider to be valuable to them?—I cannot think of any such possibility.

620. Or important?—No.

621. Are you conscious of ever having given any information to any person which you now think you ought not to have given?—No.

622. Not at all?—No.

623. Casting your mind back to the period during the war years when Russia was an ally, are you conscious of ever having said anything which, in the light of later knowledge, you feel perhaps you ought not to have said?—I cannot remember having said—I cannot remember what I would say to people almost nine or ten years ago, but as far as I know, I have never given any information or said anything of that kind which could be regarded as important or valuable.

624. Whether important or valuable, are you conscious at all of having given any information about which you now have any misgivings?—No.

625. You do know a lot of Communist Party members and Communist sympathizers, I take it?—I know a lot of people; I do not know of my own information whether they are Communists or Communist sympathizers.

626. You have no idea?—I have my own impressions of what they might be.

627. But you do know that you know a number of Communists and Communist sympathizers, I suppose?—I do not know that they are Communists.

628. THE CHAIRMAN.—But do you know that they are Communist sympathizers?—I know people who might be regarded as sympathizers, yes.

629. MR. WINDEYER.—For example, you must have met a lot of such people in your mother's home?—Whether they were Communists?

630. I am only asking you whether you met them?—I cannot answer the question unless I know. I have met people in my mother's home.

631. Do you not know very well that you have met a lot of Communists?—I am not suggesting that there is any reason why you should not, but that you have met a lot of Communists at different times?—But I cannot say that I know these people are Communists.

Witness—R. P. Throssell 2/2/55

ITEM #20

Ric and Dodie go to the Royal Commission

Brothers and sisters! I imagined them telling stories in bed after the lights went out, playing together as a big mob outside on long summer evenings. Being part of dinner chaos with everyone reaching and eating and talking with their mouths full, and there being so many kids no parent noticed.

As an only child, I was initially thrilled to be staying with my cousins – this sprawling, rambunctious family – while my parents mysteriously 'had to go to Sydney' for an even more mysterious 'while'.

My cousins lived in the bush, in a rickety weatherboard house with wide verandahs full of couches and a scramble of toys. This was the Upper Yarra, outside Melbourne, where my Uncle Ron (mum's brother) was an engineer involved in the construction of the new dam there. A far cry from the sedate Canberra suburb I came from, with its neat streets lined with alternating plums and elms.

It was 1955, and I was seven, and this was the first time I had ever stayed away from my parents. At first, it was as wonderful as I had imagined. I loved my cousins, and my energetic aunt and gentle uncle, and the feeling that things were happening all the time all around you. But when weeks turned into months, I became worried. I started losing weight, because I couldn't compete with the wild clamour at meal times. I'd been taught to be polite and wait my turn – but by then, there was very little food left. Their rule was 'first in best dressed'; anyway, it looked like that.

I noticed my uncle and aunt huddling around the radio more and more, switching it off when I came into the room. Or was I imagining this? When I asked, as I did more and more, when mum and dad were coming to collect me, they were vague – *Not long now love* – and a bit too sympathetic – *Don't worry, everything'll be all right.* When they said, *You must miss them terribly*, I suddenly realised how much I did miss them, and burst into tears. *I want to go home.*

Where were they? Why hadn't they come to get me? For the first time, I started to fear they may have abandoned me, and began desperately to wish for a bit of quiet – orderly meals with audible conversations; my own little bedroom with mum reading stories just for me. I became quiet and moody, started to resent the constant demands to be part of the relentless activities.

I was mooching on the swing the day they returned, and they couldn't find me for a while. It is one of my clearest memories – sitting there on the swing and hearing dad's voice calling me, that dear voice that I felt I hadn't heard for so long. I also remember my quiet reserved mum being so happy to see me, she did one of her famous cartwheels across the lawn.

ITEM #21

A major government enquiry into an issue of great public importance

Royal Commissions find out the truth
Mum and Dad go away for the trying
They were Definitely Not Russian Spies
I was only small and couldn't go with them

Mum and Dad go to Sydney for the listening?
Were they off to Russia? my school teacher asked
I was only small and couldn't go with them
Our greengrocer said he wouldn't serve commos

Sneaking to Russia? my schoolteacher said
No, they are in Sydney where the fairies are
The greengrocer said he wouldn't serve commos
You can't say that, my daddy's a policeman

They are going to Sydney where the ferries are
What are these commos? I think they are baddies
You can't say that, my daddy's a policeman
Betsy next door says commo's like swearing

They talk about commos, I think they are baddies
The Commission found out they weren't Russian spies
Betsy next door says commo's a bad word
Royal Commissions find out the truth

ITEM #22

A royal commissioner is not a judge, but a part-time public servant, not independent of the government. The government writes the terms of reference, and if clever enough writes them in a way that determines the outcome. The royal commissioner is a creature of the government with no constitutional protections for independence.

RICHARD ACKLAND

ITEM #23

Vladimir Petrov and the Royal Commission on Espionage

In 1951, Vladimir Petrov was officially Consul and Third Secretary in the Russian embassy in Canberra. (He was in fact a KGB colonel.)

Then, assisted by the Menzies government (who saw electoral advantage in playing the Russian threat card), the Spry-Richards security police (forerunners of ASIO), and the Australian media, Petrov and his wife Evdokia set out to parade themselves as 'master spies', alleging a 'vast Soviet spy ring in Australia', all of whom they would expose. This was in return for the offer of asylum in Australia – in Barrister E. F. Hill's words, *'a promise of eternal comfort'* – and £5,000.

The subsequent Royal Commission on Espionage set up by the Menzies government and presided over by three handpicked judges, Justices Owen, Philp and Ligertwood, 'saw the ugly methods of McCarthyism brought to Australia.' Victor Windeyer QC appeared to assist for the Commission, and Frank Louat QC appeared for Ric and Dorothy Throssell.

ITEM #24

Reading through his statements, I find it quite astonishing that Petrov was given any credence. His statements are full of contradictions and inconsistencies. There are also some interesting 'facts' which he could not have obtained from the usual sources.

Statements of V Petrov 7/2/1954 and 12/9/1954

> Early in 1952 the Committee of Information came under the control of M. G. B. (Ministry of State Security). At this time PAKHOMOV, the Tass representative in Australia, was the representative of this Organisation and I was in charge of M. V. D... [PAKHOMOV] was to be my assistant...

> [He] told me that he believed Throssell was an agent of the Soviet Union.

> Early in 1952 I forwarded a list of the officers of the Australian Department of External Affairs to Moscow. This list included the name of THROSSELL...

> A short time after this I received a special cable from M. V. D. Moscow stating that the man Throssell... is known to us (M. V. D.) by the code name of FERRO... [and that] he was very important...

> The cable indicated that the members of this special group were not aware [contradicting his previous statement] the information was being obtained for Moscow.

This was contradicted in the Venona decrypts, where Throssell is described **as having no importance to Moscow.**

> The cable gave a special order for us to work out a plan whereby Mr KISLYTSIN could personally contact THROSSELL and this plan was to be sent to Moscow for approval before action could be taken...

Kislitsyn's functions were to exploit the Diplomatic corps and the Department of External Affairs, and he had a list of names with which to do it, and Throssell's name was not there.

The information about Throssell's code name could not have been given to Petrov by Russia. The code name only came to light with the Venona decrypts and, as a defector, always possibly a Soviet plant, he could never be allowed to know of the Venona decrypts. But if the information was fed to him and replayed as his own evidence, the possibility of its source being revealed would be safeguarded against.

Throssell believed that Ron Richards, as Deputy Director of ASIO, would have had access to the decrypts, had a long-term grudge against him and also spent considerable time with Petrov before and after the time of his defection.

Given all of the above, the final paragraph of Petrov's statement is astonishing:

> **I cannot say who actually passed the information to the Embassy** because neither the cable nor any other material which passed through my hands showed this.

ITEM # 25

499. THE CHAIRMAN.—I think so. Why not, Mr. Windeyer?

500. MR. WINDEYER.—Yes, Your Honour.

"The Communist Party here had a group of External Affairs Officers who were giving them official information.

The members of the group were bringing out copies of official documents, which they gave to a Communist Party member.

The Party man gave the documents to Mr. Makarov at the Soviet Embassy.

The documents described the Australian foreign policy and also contained a lot of information about American and English foreign policy.

I do not know the name of the Party man who at that time reported to Makarov but his code name was 'Klode'— (phonetically this is CLAUDE). One of Klode's group was Ric Throssell, an officer of the Dept. of External Affairs.

Witness—V. M. Petrov 1/2/55

1989

Throssell had a code name 'Ferro'. Throssell is the son of Katherine Susannah Pritchard, the Australian writer.

He has served abroad for External Affairs in the Soviet and also in South America.

He is not active now—he is very still—I think he is afraid.

Moscow sent me a cable to me during 1953—it was in June—instructing me that he was a very important man and that I had to arrange personal contact with him for Mr. Kislytsin.

Kislytsin invited him to the Soviet 7th November reception in Canberra in 1953—he attended but did not stay long—we also invited him to a film night at the Embassy, but he did not answer and did not attend.

I do not know how many reports he made, but Moscow regarded him as very important to them—I know his information was regarded as important."

501. Then, Your Honours, it goes on to another matter. Perhaps I might ask Mr. Petrov to look at this, if he can read it in English, otherwise it can be translated to him by Mr. Birse. I will put a pencil mark on page 14 opposite the paragraph I want Mr. Petrov to read.

502. DR. LOUAT.—Is this part of what you have read?

503. MR. WINDEYER.—No. (The witness reads.) (To the witness) Mr. Petrov, you expressed there what you describe as your opinion?—Yes.

In a statement to ASIO on 21 May 1954, Petrov writes that, in early 1952, he

> ...received a special cable from M.V.D. Moscow. The cable stated that 'Ferro' THROSSELL was very important; that during the war years he gave very important information to 'Klode' (KLODE) who was the leader of a special group.

During World War II, Throssell was a soldier in New Guinea in 1943 before receiving a diplomatic cadetship to join the Department of External Affairs in 1943. He was 21. He was only in Canberra (with alleged access to External Affairs files) as a raw recruit, and for less than two years. In that time, he courted and married his first wife, Bea. He was posted to Moscow in 1945, where he stayed less than a year because of her tragic sudden death.

In 1953, Moscow directed Kislitsyn to meet Throssell at a reception at the Soviet Embassy. Throssell, it appeared, was to be 're-activated'. Accordingly, he was invited to a screening of Russian films; but he neither attended nor responded to the invitation. He was then invited, along with other members of the Department of External Affairs as cover, to the National Day reception on 7 November 1953. He attended, but no acquaintance was made with Kislitsyn, who spoke little English, 'had not previously seen THROSSELL and did not have his description.'

Petrov concluded his statement with the comment that 'Moscow was advised of the result of the operation and no further instructions were received from Moscow.'

Despite Kislitsyn's failure to contact, let alone re-activate, Throssell, he continued to believe – according to a statement to ASIO by Evdokia Petrov on 28 May 1954 – that Throssell 'had been an active and successful agent for the Soviet, both in Australia and abroad.' She stated that it was primarily Kislitsyn who gave her the impression that Throssell was 'useful' to the Soviet Union when stationed in Moscow. Neither her nor her husband's statements yield any details of how long or in what way 'Ferro' gave useful intelligence. She also added that she was certain that he was 'an active agent for the Soviet in Rio de Janeiro, Brazil, and giving valuable information.'

ITEM #26

'An active agent' passing 'valuable information' from Rio

Rio was the end of the tramline. In the end there was no getting away from it. My three years in Brazil had been some sort of exotic exile. There was nothing of any importance to Australia in the work of the Australian legation [in Rio]. Once perhaps, the Brazilian government's influence with the Latin American bloc had meant something to us, but any prospects of trade had long since disappeared.

My efforts to be taken seriously as the representative of Australia were shaken when I heard that myself and the junior commonwealth diplomats were referred to as 'the kindergarten'.

Ric was 27. He responded by attempting to grow a moustache!

ITEM #27

Victor Windeyer (QC appearing for the Commission):

> the Commission must in no way interfere with 'freedom of thought'. Individuals must be protected from 'malicious gossip or ignorant speculation'.

Point by point the lawyer takes Petrov through the story. Petrov blandly agrees my name has not been on any Moscow documents, the list of contacts, the instructions to cultivate External Affairs people, the plans for the MVD in Canberra, the names left by his predecessor.

He made no attempt to contact me at the November 7th reception, when I fail to turn up to a film. That was Kislytsin's task, he says Kislytsin has not tried to contact me either.

After that surely no one is going to believe I am some kind of Soviet spy.

ITEM #28

Frank Louat

597. In this case evidence has been given by Throssell, evidence which, in my submission, is of a very striking kind. The Commission had before it a

Dr. Louat, Q.C. 7/2/55

man who, I think, may have commended himself as one with a frank, clear, and sensitive mind, and a high degree of intellectual integrity, a man on whose word full confidence could be placed. He is obviously an unusual man, a man of brilliance and capacity, a man who comes of unusual parents—and if he had some leftish atmosphere from his mother, at all events he also got moral courage from both of them. I think Your Honours may have thought that in all your respective long experiences you had never seen evidence given more straightforwardly and frankly.

ITEM #29

In 1955, Arthur Tange, Secretary of the Department of External Affairs, wrote a long letter to Spry, saying that, on the information available, he saw no reason to bar Throssell from access to classified information. Tange referred to 'the law relating to the use against a witness before the Royal Commission of any evidence given by him.' He seems to have worried that it would look as though Throssell had been denied a security clearance simply because of his appearance at the Royal Commission. This would have been an obvious injustice, because the commissioners promised that witnesses would not be punished for appearing.

ITEM #30

Tange, Throssell, Spry, Bailey

> … T. was regarded as a serious security risk without any act on his part…Throssell was trapped. As Spry laid out ASIO policy: reasons must not be given to the person why they are a security risk, not even that they were a security risk, but that they 'failed to obtain a security clearance' (and this was told to the person only if compelled to do so. This was done so only as a last resort.)

ITEM #31

When the evidence doesn't fit the (foregone) conclusion

In 1953, when the two ASIO agents came to our home in Canberra to interview dad, apparently they were not impressed with his deportment, but concluded: 'Throssell is a **loyal subject and is not a security risk.**'

ASIO later described this meeting as 'not a very productive event'; they had no success finding out about his communist background.

ITEM #32

ASIO has problems with the Royal Commission

The Liberal Government and ASIO planned to use the 1955 Royal Commission to investigate **and expose** communist espionage (assuming guilt before it was investigated).

Not only that, it was assuming guilt despite the fact that there was evidence to the contrary.

Their challenge was to protect information 'that might come out in the royal commission hearings'; this referred to information contained in the Venona decrypts – even the fact that Venona existed. In fact, according to Horner's Official History of ASIO, the commissioners were to be 'indoctrinated into the Venona program', so they would have known Venona had 'provided no evidence that Throssell had given classified information to the Russians.'

Despite this 'indoctrination', ASIO still experienced some difficulty with senior counsel, Windeyer. When Throssell denied divulging official material to unauthorised personnel, 'Windeyer had failed to make the most of this and other opportunities.'

Colonel Spry was then authorised to instruct Windeyer on the general lines to be followed, and he suggested the order of witnesses in the light of ASIO's investigations.

They also objected to the fact that Windeyer wanted to call witnesses arbitrarily, based on his **own study of Petrov's documents.**

ASIO had in fact set up a special section within the organisation known as the Royal Commission Section, with Ron Richards as controller. Most of the summaries and chronologies of the Petrov defection which were used by the Royal Commission **came from ASIO itself.**

ITEM #33

MI5 has problems with the Royal Commission

Despite this, the Commission found Petrov's evidence about Throssell all 'remote hearsay assertions' and that 'in face of Throssell's denial, it would be wrong to hold that he had been a member of "Klod's group" or that he had wittingly given away any information.'

But, of course, MI5 had already made up its mind. Hamblen, the MI5 security liaison officer, reported that Windeyer 'may be a good Equity lawyer, but his technique as a cross-examiner **of communists** leaves much to be desired.'

After reading the report of the Royal Commission, one senior MI5 officer was able to observe that: 'There can be **no reasonable doubt** that Throssell was at one time an active and conscious spy.' The case officer concluded that a **'most unfortunate result'** had been reached with regard to Ric Throssell: 'he was virtually cleared of all suspicion'.

> It goes on for two days – the familiar questions. I have been twice asked by ASIO the same list of names: people I know, people I have never met, colleagues in the department, people at my mother's flat, names I have never heard of, lists of Russian officials, people I can only guess about, the same questions about work and friends…

ITEM #34

Justice Philp – Royal Commission

> [W]e have no direct concern with the effect on his career. In this regard if his career was affected, he would have his rights of appeal at law to the tribunal in the Public Service.

ITEM #35

A Spook's Second Thoughts

A Fictional Encounter

GILMOUR: Did you ever think we might have made a mistake?

THOMPSON: God no. Look at the family: Mum's a dyed-in-the-wool commo, trots round the place spruiking the stuff; he's in External Affairs (handy...) and they post him to bloody Russia!

And look at the lifestyle! They're outsiders, bohemians – vacuum the carpets at three in the morning. They live outside the rules, arty wankers. He writes *plays* for god's sake. One was even about an affair between an American and a Russian... Say no more.

GILMOUR: Sort of like Romeo and Juliet...

THOMPSON: What are you, some sort of arty wanker too? And then there's the wife, been seen at some of those commo parties, been seen talking to Wally Clayton. He's a self-confessed...

GILMOUR: Doesn't make her one though.

THOMPSON: What do you reckon? Would anyone but a total sympathiser be seen at these things? (Other than us pretending to be, of course!)

GILMOUR: Both deny it vehemently, whereas Clayton is proud of himself.

THOMPSON: Of course Throssell would deny it. He's got to watch his cushy public service job, doesn't he? Though we've made sure he doesn't get anywhere with it, no career path for him. Can't have a known commo—

GILMOUR: But he's not a known commo. The Royal Commission said he wasn't one. Said the Russians weren't at all interested in him, regardless of his mother.

THOMPSON: Look, whose side are you on?

We know, that's what matters. The Royal Commission was stacked with leftie lawyers anyway. They wouldn't know what they were talking about.

GILMOUR: But a Royal Commission? They're supposed to be the ultimate in finding out the real facts of a case.

THOMPSON: Mate, I'm worried about you. Too many questions. Too much concern for the fate of a fuckin' menace to our democracy.

Better watch out, or I'll start a file on you.

VENONA DECRYPTS

The Moscow connection

New claims have emerged that a spy network run by Australia's Communist Party during World War II passed valuable Allied secrets to Moscow. In this extract from their new book, Desmond Ball and David Horner argue that this act may have prolonged the Pacific war and cost the lives of Australian servicemen

The Group

Wally Clayton (KLOD)

BORN New Zealand 1906. Moved to Australia. Joined the Communist Party of Australia in 1933, became full-time party apparatchik, went underground 1940-41, first contacted Soviets 1943, passed on secrets until 1949. Went back underground when his network was blown.

Fodor NOSOV (TEKhNIK)

JOURNALIST with TASS newsagency recruited by NKGB as Sydney contact from 1943-50, operating from flat in Darlinghurst.

Ian Milner (BUR)

BELONGED to Friends of Soviet University at Canterbury University, NZ, from 1930-33. He was a Rhodes Scholar at Oxford from 1933-37, visited Moscow in 1934, political science lecturer Melbourne University from 1940-44, secret CPA member from 1940, joined External Affairs 1945, left for UN Security Council Secretariat at the end of 1946, defected to Czechoslovakia in 1950, worked as academic and undercover informant for Czech intelligence. Died in Prague 1991.

Katherine Susannah Prichard (ACADEMICIAN)

BORN 1883, became well-known journalist and then novelist, increasingly of socialist-realist bent. Foundation member of CPA in 1920, later on CPA central committee, and loyal party member till her death in 1969.

Alfred Hughes (BEN)

NSW POLICE-man from 1924. He joined Military Police Intelligence in 1940. He transferred to Security Service 1942, becoming chief of counter-espionage watching the CPA. He returned to NSW police in 1945. He had been a secret CPA member since 1932.

Frances Bernie (SESTRA)

JOINED CPA in 1941, typist in office of External Affairs minister H.V. Evatt 1944-46, confessed to ASIO she had passed material to Clayton after Billy Graham evangelical meeting in 1959.

Semyen Makharov (EFIM) NKGB

RESIDENT in Canberra at Soviet Legation from 1943-49, initial cover as "clerk" then third and second secretary. His residency took over the whole top floor of the Soviet Embassy, and included offices, cipher section, safe, dark room, incinerator, and reading room.

Jim Hill (TOURIST)

CPA member from 1938, in Moonee Ponds branch. He joined External Affairs in 1945 and was rapidly promoted, being posted to UN mission, transferred to London in 1950 and grilled by MI5. He returned to Canberra in 1951 with security clearance reduced. He left public service in 1953 to practise law in Melbourne.

ITEM #36

Crypto-analysts read more than 200 cables between Canberra and Moscow revealing names and code names of about a dozen Australians who had 'provided information to the Soviet Union or in some way had come to the notice of the Soviets.' Dad clearly fell into this latter category, listing the three references to him in the documents. Two of them were factual, common knowledge: he was the son of Katharine Susannah Prichard, and he had a junior posting to Moscow. The third – a query as to whether, given his communist mother, Moscow 'could use him' – is obviously the one that interested ASIO. There was no affirming response and no mention of him divulging classified information. In fact, if they were still querying 'using' him, this was surely proof that he hadn't already handed over information.

It seems that the mere appearance of his name in the Venona files and his having a code name – FERRO – was enough to convict him in the eyes of ASIO. Colonel Spry apparently built his whole case against my father on the fact that he was 'named' by Venona, ignoring the fact that he was also exonerated by Venona...

ITEM #37

In a statement referring to the case of Nina and Clem Christensen, Petrov revealed that being given a code name **did not necessarily mean you were assumed to be a spy**.

> I did not know that Nina M. CHRISTENSEN had a code name until I opened Envelope 'N' shortly before my departure from the Soviet Embassy when I saw that she was known by the code name 'EVA.'

ITEM #38

David Horner argues that:

> The Venona decrypts provide no evidence that Throssell had given classified information to the Russians. But ASIO also needed to consider the decrypts that mentioned Throssell in the context of all the other decrypts which showed how Makarov and Clayton were organising their spy ring.

ITEM #39

There are critics of the 'evidence' provided by Venona. In the US, Victor Navasky, editor and publisher of *The Nation*, claims that:

> Venona material has been used as much to distort as to expand our understanding of the cold war…[the files] are potential timebombs of misinformation.

He commented on the list of 349 Americans identified by Venona:

> The reader is left with the implication – unfair and unproven – that every name on the list was involved in espionage, and as a result, otherwise careful historians and mainstream journalists now routinely refer to Venona as proof that many hundreds of Americans were part of a red spy network.

In his defence of the listed people, he said:

> There were a lot of exchanges of information among people of good will… Most of these exchanges were innocent and within the law.

ITEM #40

In Australia, Phillip Deery raised similar issues:

> While some cables were conclusive, others must be treated with caution and circumspection. Venona is fragmentary, raw and one-way intelligence data. The cable-senders could exaggerate and the cable-receivers could misinterpret. Not surprisingly, all the transcripts revealed was what had already been exposed by the Royal Commission – that the Soviets had no more than a wary interest in the son of a well-known communist.

ITEM #41

The release of the Venona decrypts gave dad a hope that he had found the reason for ASIO's persistent refusal to abide by the findings of the 1955 Royal Commission and grant him a security clearance. He saw the information it released as *untying the last knot.*

He believed that **the fact the Soviet ciphers had been broken could not be allowed to be known or guessed at by the Russians**...and that this was why ASIO couldn't let it be known that, contrary to their own files, the Russians were not interested in Ric Throssell. Maintaining the illusion that he was a spy for the Russians kept the knowledge of the code breaking safe.

Unbeknownst to my father (or to ASIO?) at the time, there is now evidence that the Russians knew that the codes had been broken as early as 1948. William Weisband, a double agent working for the Soviets, first alerted the Russians to the fact that the Venona project was on the verge of success. While Weisband was able to divulge the US's cryptoanalytic success, it was British master spy Kim Philby who regularly received actual translations and analyses of the codes.

Weisband's role as a Soviet agent was not discovered by counterintelligence until 1950, by which time the damage had been done.

Weisband was a real spy. A ridgy-didge, dyed-in-the-wool, self-confessed double agent. Yet he completely escaped prosecution for espionage! The authorities feared that a trial would divulge yet more information to Soviet intelligence. He remained in the US for the rest of his life, quietly working as an insurance salesman.

Basically, his story is the opposite of the Throssell case, in which an innocent man was forced to live under a cloud for the rest of his life in case declaring his innocence would compromise intelligence gathering. Or was it because it might have exposed the utter incompetence of ASIO and Colonel Spry and the fact that the Russians had the last laugh on them after all?

ITEM #42

reputation

n. the beliefs or opinions that are generally held about someone or something. a widespread belief that someone or something has a particular characteristic.

ITEM #43

Despite these inconclusive findings, the release of the Venona transcripts still encouraged the Cold War warriors to crawl out from the woodwork:

> On October 3 1996 The Courier Mail publishes a sensational front-page story referencing me by name as 'the suspected Soviet agent' beneath photos of Evatt, Petrov, Burgess and Philby:
>
> **SPY FILES REVEAL AUSTRALIA'S ROLE IN RUSSIAN INTELLIGENCE RING**
>
> The Australian follows the next day with a front-page banner headline:
>
> **CONFIRMED – OUR SOVIET SPIES**
>
> and a photo of Richard Prichard Throssell [sic] together with Walter Seddon Clayton.

ITEM #44

Excerpts from letter from Ric Throssell to his lawyer Thena Kyprianou in late October 1966.

An apology appeared in *The Australian* buried on p. 14. *The Courier Mail* did not apologise at all.

Dear Thena,

Following are items I suggest for inclusion in a letter to the Courier Mail seeking an immediate apology and correction:

I find the article on page 1 of the Courier Mail of 3rd October in which I am referred to in the context of the Venona tapes and your interpretations of them defamatory, offensive, grossly damaging to my reputation and prejudicial to my opportunities to secure publication as a writer.

The article omits reference in the Venona tapes to the reluctance of the Soviet authorities to establish contact with me because of my mother's well-known and proudly acknowledged associations; it implies improper motives to my posting to the Australian Legation in Moscow as a third Secretary in 1945; it omits reference to my clearance at the Royal Commission into Espionage in 1955, and ignores the fact that I remained an officer of the Department of Foreign Affairs until my retirement as Assistant Secretary in 1985...

Documents released under the Freedom of Information Act later revealed that Ric Throssell had been under surveillance, as the son of Katharine Susannah Prichard, since his school days, and that evidence about him given by Vladimir Petrov was explicitly suggested to him by RG Richards, Deputy Director of ASIO. ASIO documents now on public access in The Australian archives substantiate these facts...

DOROTHY

ITEM #45

EILEEN DOROTHY THROSSELL, sworn:

726. MR. PAPE.—Mrs. Throssell, your name is Eileen Dorothy Throssell?—Yes.

727. You are a married woman and the wife of Mr. Throssell who gave evidence here yesterday, I think?—Yes.

728. You reside with him in Canberra?—Yes.

729. Can you tell me when you were married?—Yes; in October 1947.

730. And prior to your marriage was your maiden name Jordan?—Yes.

731. You are, I think, a graduate of the University of Melbourne, aren't you?—Yes.

732. And when did you take your degree at Melbourne?—In 1944.

733. THE CHAIRMAN.—It was a degree in what?—Arts.

Witnesses—C. W. Dakin, E. D. Throssell 4/2/55

ASIO's other suspect as Clayton's mole in the department of post-war reconstruction was Dorothy Throssell (code name DZhON).

ITEM #46

Deciphering code

Dorothy Jordan alias DZhON
Russian agent, Soviet spy
Clandestine meetings
with sinister strangers
brown paper parcels
on lonely park benches?

Dorothy Jordan is a philosopher
She always asks questions,
challenges givens.
Unthinkable, any mindless allegiance,
unthinkable, any slavish adherence
to some rigid doctrine.

Dorothy Jordan, snow-silent, owl-wise
blending with shadows, cowering from crowds.
She found her soul-mate: mind and heart.
But this man had a mother – the red witch of the west.
This man had a mother –
contagious they said.

Now these creeping brown men,
small of brain, slight of heart,
make up their stories,
sell them as truth.
Portray her as some Mata Hari,
portray her like that dumb Evdokia?

Why was it DZhON?
(We know they can't spell.)
A savoury condiment
to have on the side?
She was nobody's side-kick – no one could tell her,
She was nobody's side-kick,
and nobody's fool.

Her name was not DZhON
it was Dorothy Eileen –
green Irish hills,
and wild native gardens
painting and dreaming and loving her kids.
Who was this DZhON? Who was this DZhON?
She wasn't my mother.

ITEM #47

Sonnet for Dorothy

She says *I think therefore I am*
Dorothy, BA, fulfils a dream.
The world is hers, and she has plans:
to search for Truth – it's lost it seems.
Words, ideas and asking why –
believing more in those who seek
than they who always claim to find.
So many questions, afraid to speak,
this solemn girl on the edge of life.
Appears so cool, has come so far
from the wild bush kid who courted strife.
Once this was earth, it's now a star.
So now what does the future hold –
this world, life, this defining scroll?

I know Dodie belonged to the Communist Party and the Labour Club while she was at University.

Now someone says she has taken papers from External Affairs, handed them to CPA headquarters.

It is the same old thing – blind accusations. There is nothing you can do but deny them.

We are both to be called before the Royal Commission.

At least we can be together.

Methodically she is led over the same paths. She replies quietly, briefly, without any of the qualifications and hesitations that mark her accuser.

She admits she joined the Communist Party at University. Her membership lapsed when she left. She agrees she had known the Tribune correspondent, but there were no regular meetings, no stolen documents, no secrets.

ITEM #48

Those conversations we didn't have

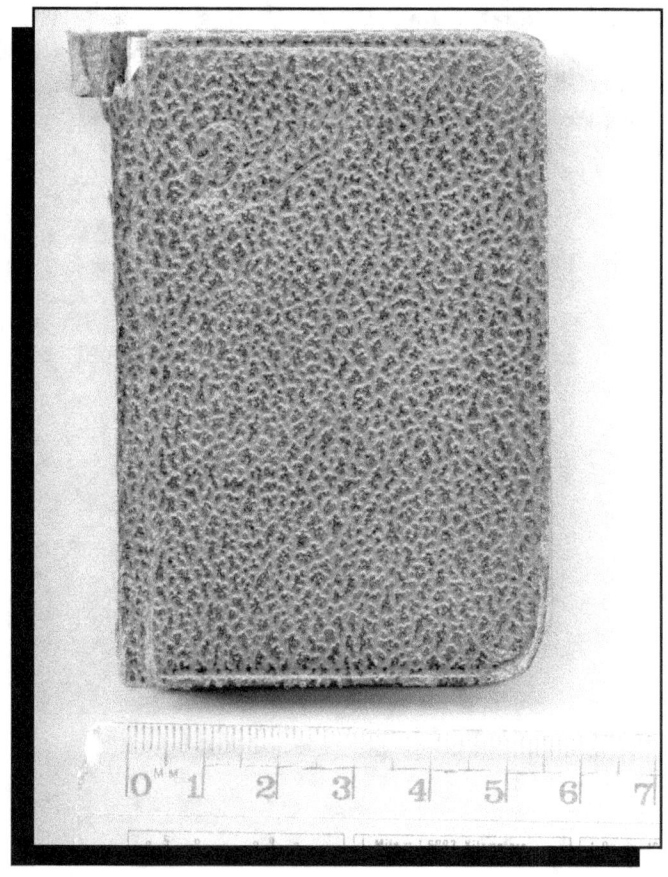

DIARY TO SCALE

Dorothy Jordan – Melbourne University Philosophy Department

First class honours 1945. Freethought Society, Labour Club, Eureka Youth League.

> Once I wrote:
>
> *Quietly beautiful*
>
> *and beautifully quiet.*
>
> *So giving of self*
>
> *that sometimes*
>
> *you seemed not to exist.*
>
> But I found you
>
> in your diary – 1942
>
> the mother I never knew.

DOROTHY:

March 15 QUESTION
People are beginning to talk about things
to question and query and think.
That's something good to come from this war –

> My mum, the housewife –
>
> What you could have taught me! What a time to be living and writing and questioning! And how many people analysed it as much as you did?

April 14 FREEDOM
Went to the Freethought Society meeting
Mr. Barbour spoke on 'Freedom'
Still couldn't pluck up courage to speak
Am extremely annoyed with myself –

> Always the philosopher, always questioning. How frustrating not being able to voice it all.

April 15 RUSSIA
Still didn't speak at Labour Club meeting
Dorothy Gibson spoke on 'Youth in Russia'
Quite good, but not so enthusiastic about Russia,
still interested, but not mad about it –

> I can hear your voice!
>
> All those conversations we didn't have about the Russian spy you weren't.

May 12
Free Thought Society on 'HG Wells the Scientist'
Yours truly said nothing as usual –

> Beautifully quiet!
>
> Now I know your anguish
>
> 'Shy' was defeat, 'quiet' was failure.

May 15 SHY

Must try and conquer my inhibitions
and achieve self-realisation –

> My sister and I thought you
> didn't speak much because Dad
> smothered you.
>
> Maybe you welcomed his voice.

July 9 EUREKA!
Eureka Youth League meeting
Didn't say anything and didn't mix very well –

> You told me about these meetings.
> This is where you learned to be
> such a good poker player. Guerrilla
> training in the day, strategy and
> tactics in the night.

June 21
I wish I could get more confidence
in myself. Generally life would be
so much happier

> How could you have no confidence?
> Extremely bright, extremely beautiful.
> Maybe too much philosophy. Too
> many questions without answers.

July 23 MARRIAGE
Bill still insisted
that he would rather
have married me, but I remain firm
in my opposition to marriage

> Mum!
>
> Why didn't you ever tell me?
>
> We were so alike! But I suppose my stance as 'ferocious feminist' made it not so easy to talk to me. After all, you did end up 'selling out' and marrying Dad.
>
> God, I curse my brash self-assurance.

March 10 IDEAL LOVE
My emotional life still confused.
Can't decide what constitutes
ideal love and if love is above
race, colour or creed
or whether they are part of it all?

> Ever the philosopher. You didn't just accept that lust equals love and assume that the first one was the 'ideal'.

February 16
Singapore has fallen.
Goodness knows what will happen now.
We might all be Japanese serfs
before long, or else blown off
the face of the earth.

> What a frightening time it would have been. Impossible for us to imagine.

April 7 DEMOCRACY

Went to a debate tonight – 'That democracy is doomed who-ever wins the war'

> And yet you were still thinking and debating. Then what did domesticity do to you a short while later? Married woman, of course you had to resign your job in the public service. A brand new baby in a brand new suburb. No political meetings there.

April 16 FAMILY

Spent the evening at home with the family arguing about war, pacifism, freedom. No conclusion reached.

> Of course not, you were the only progressive thinker in the family, but still you tried.
>
> First mention of family too –
>
> No plan for your own then and at twenty-five...

June 11

Went to 'The 49th Parallel'. Acted well, but too much obvious propaganda – the splendid and heroic allies and the bad inhuman Nazis

> Lucky ASIO didn't read your diaries. How dare you challenge the black and white view of history, tantamount to supporting the enemy!

July 29 GUERRILLA

Went to guerrilla war practice on Monday,

was in Frank's party. Chap spoke on China today,

quite good

> I used to have a book called *Tania the Unforgettable Guerrilla* (fighting beside Che in Bolivia). And to think, there was my mum, training in the Dandenongs preparing for the revolution.

July 15 ARMY

Lounged about at home today. Read and thought.

Went down and met Dave at 8.30.

I can't get used to him in uniform.

He seems to have changed.

Has the cold air of the army.

It seems to have hardened him

> And who were they – Bill and Dave and Gavin – all who wanted to marry you? So hard to think of my mum and 'other men'. I'm so glad you stayed committed to your position on marriage (at that stage anyway).

April 15 BEER

Went out with Gavin

Walked around St. Kilda looking for beer

but couldn't find any.

Finished the beer we had

and settled down for a pretty good time.

Got home at 6.25. No all-night trams!

My mum, the rager –

who would have thought?

But I suppose my daughters don't
know quite how wild I was when I was
young. Must burn my diaries!

March 16

Had my hair set tonight

Ah, so there was some

female frippery. But that's
the extent of it –

no mention of clothes,
cooking, gossip,

the surface of things.

March 17 SELF

Monday reaction again

the calm after the storm.

After the weekend I seem to revert

to another self, and become the weekly me

though bits of the weekend drift back

to remind me. I can never quite lose myself in anything,

the rationalist in me always remains

> The old heart vs head dichotomy... So hard when you feel yourself split in two. But when you found Dad did they finally come together? And did the articulate and extrovert Ric save your tongue-tied self? Was someone who adored you, and did all the talking, your idea of bliss?
>
> I think so, I hope so.
>
> My darling Mum, whom I really didn't know –
>
> All those conversations
>
> we didn't have...

SEPTEMBER 1942
Wednesday 16

Lect. & Tut. tonight - didn't say anything as usual - saw Bill quite a lot today - he still gives me a thrill - didn't go to rehearsal tonight - first time I've missed - marvellous sudden meeting today - evangelic union - Canon Hammond on "Reasonableness" (hardly) Edwards as usual challenged the speaker & rest of meeting consisted in arguments (etc) then still haven't heard from Jack.

SEPTEMBER 1942
Thursday 17

Went to Engsoc meeting tonight - almost as bad as first time I went though perhaps a bit better - still didn't say anything - went with Jay - had lunch with Alan Killop - met 2 friends of his Lionel & Keith - latter extremely interesting - learnt quite a lot politically - has a very broad outlook on communism. Harry came home yesterday with asthma but stice today - very bad - haven't heard from him yet -

ITEM #49

What a strange state of affairs when innocent friendships and casual encounters are seen as sinister.

Should I now question these people I had presumed were friends? I think not.

DOROTHY THROSSELL'S DIARY

ITEM #50

Romanticism

Our family didn't believe in Mothers Day. Dad called it Shops' Day.

'Buy mum a kitchen appliance to keep capitalism and patriarchy happy' was the view he passed on to us kids.

Dad always said every day should be Mothers Day. Every day, mum got a cup of tea in bed in the morning before he went off to work, even on weekends. Later, my partner and I amended the regime: I got a cup of tea in bed on weekdays because he had to leave earlier than I did, but I brought him tea in bed on the weekends, when we both wanted to sleep in.

And dad didn't need a special day for gifts – not even birthdays. He would arrive home out of the blue with presents for mum: perfume, jewellery or books. Definitely not household appliances. And he certainly didn't need to be told what books to buy for her; not the usual Mothers Day offerings: *Home decorating for the creative housewife* or *The queen and her corgis* or some nice motherly romance.

I only ever heard my parents argue fiercely once. It was so alarming, I got out of bed to investigate, and they both stopped yelling and stared shamefacedly at me in my nightie, with my big shocked eyes. Normally, mum could do no wrong in dad's eyes, but my sister says the fight was because dad wanted to come home from a party and mum wanted to stay…obviously dad prevailed. It was the sixties, after all.

In her last years, mum developed terrible leg ulcers which had to be dressed every day. Dad devoted himself to her care, getting angry with me for suggesting that he would qualify for a carer's pension.

> **I don't do this for money, I do it for love.**

When she was diagnosed with a terminal brain tumour, he couldn't bear to live without her. They had a pact. They'd go together. And they did.

ITEM # 51

Australian Security Intelligence Organization Act 1979

No. 113 of 1979

TABLE OF PROVISIONS

PART I—PRELIMINARY

Section
1. Short title
2. Commencement
3. Repeal
4. Interpretation
5. Meaning of subversion when not of foreign origin

PART II—THE ORGANIZATION AND THE DIRECTOR-GENERAL

6. Continuance of Organization
7. Director-General
8. Control of Organization
9. Term of office of Director-General
10. Remuneration and allowances of Director-General
11. Leave of absence
12. Resignation
13. Termination of appointment
14. Acting Director-General
15. Appointment of a Judge as Director-General
16. Rights of public servant appointed as Director-General

PART III—FUNCTIONS AND POWERS OF ORGANIZATION

Division 1—General

17. Functions of Organization
18. Communication of intelligence, &c.
19. Co-operation with other authorities
20. Special responsibility of Director-General in relation to functions of Organization
21. Leader of Opposition to be kept informed on security matters

Division 2—Special Powers

22. Interpretation
23. References to Minister
24. Exercise of authority under warrants

15087/79 Cat. No. 79 5198 X—Recommended retail price 80c

spy

n.(pl. -ies) 1. a person employed by a government or other organisation to collect and report secret information on an enemy or competitor. 2. a person who observes others secretly v. (-ies, ied) 3. be a spy (spy on) observe furtively.

ITEM #52

Damn them all and the money's good

You'd have to think big
for the world – not small
for one country. You'd have to believe
that you know what is wrong.

Passion for principle, not place,
not the one you live in.
You eschew nationalism:
flag-draped hoodlums and bristling generals.

If I knew something that would serve my country but would harm another, I would never reveal it, for I am a citizen of humanity first and by necessity, and a citizen of France second, and only by accident.

MONTESQUIEU

You're only here because it's where
you were born – a man, a woman
(your mum and dad – do you care?)
It could have been anywhere.

Maybe you love another country –
Russia, for instance, or Israel.
They've got the answer, you're sure,
so sure, you are theirs.

So sure, you must be certain
that theirs is the way, and you have
Truth, Justice (and sometimes god)
on your side.

So sure, you give them your life:
your real life, where your heart is.
In your other life, your sham life
you are just a stranger.

*You betrayed me. How could you have betrayed me? How **could** you? How **could** you?*

GASKIN TO HIS LOVER, ANTHONY BLUNT

No one knows the real you there –
not your mother, your child, your
closest friend.
(Is there such a thing?)
In this world you're alone, with your
huge secret load.

So for all the bad press, you are selfless,
giving your life to that big idea –
your secret solitary life
where all pleasure is pretence.

There are great occasions in which some men are called to great services in the doing of which they are excused from the common rule of morality.

ATTRIBUTED TO OLIVER CROMWELL

Is that how it always is?
Maybe it isn't love for a country,
a dream for the future, even a big idea.
Maybe it's hate, and you seethe with fury,

If I had to choose between betraying my friend and betraying my country, I hope I would have the guts to betray my country.

ANTHONY BLUNT, QUOTING E. M. FORSTER

fury at your country's cant,
hypocrisy, mindless materialism.
So much, you will sell their secrets
such as they are

to the highest bidder –
An ideological mercenary.
Damn them all, and the money's good.
This country understands you now.

ITEM #53

Petrov Putting in

Petrov said how did it go – did they talk about us? He got an answer that everything went alright. He subsequently explained to me that there was a meeting at the embassy and very often he said, the bastards try to 'put somebody in' and they talk about each other. He said he despised the system of 'putting each other in.'

I suppose 'putting people in'/my job/but you don't expect it from so-called comrades at embassy/they say on same side/in russia of course a lot of 'putting in'/factories not meeting targets/comrades reading banned books/old teachers with wrong history/sometimes may be innocent/just bad timing you know/but important tales for telling/ these enemies of state/I did good job there/so they send to australia/ more 'putting in'/balts and croats/more enemies of the people/australia is good place/they have as we say volia here/lots of wine whiskey/good looking women/easy women/cafes clubs good whiskey/all the women

I have friend here already/pole named bialoguski/michael/very smooth/ very smart/comrade I'm sure/we have some good schemes together/ money schemes/duty free whiskey/getting free charging money/more whiskey/paying back traitors at embassy/they make life hell/more and more/telling tales to moscow about me/moscow wants me back/lifanov kovaliev/try to force me/those bastards/putting me in/supposed to be comrades/I not want this/australia life good/ but I must do duty/they watch my house/I frightened what they do/don't trust no one no more but michael/he has plan/talks about chicken farm/chicken farm called *dream acres*/could be good dream/I'm peasant you see/this my roots/so/chicken farm in australia/with the volia/yes, I think/michael he help with money/he says stay in australia proper/defection/official money/regular/for help their spy agency/think this good idea/but no asylum for nothing/oh no/price of course/they want putting in of australian spies/funny eh?/they spying for moscow/and I put them in/some I never know/not even comrades/maybe not even spies/ but australian spy catchers want names/likely names/man with communist mother/never heard of her/maybe not even a comrade/ man works in sensitive area/likely link/richards says he is/likely name/what was name?/throstle/something like that/never heard of him/just likely name/wrong place maybe/then money offered/give more names/get more money/so what would you do?/5000 pounds? of course I take/likely become most likely/most likely become certain/so close/these important tales for telling/help my new country/help save my neck/putting people in/is my job you know

ITEM #54

who wants to be a russian spy?

it's not that I care if they call me pro-russian
those days we all loved the workers' paradise

chandeliers in the metro, miners at the bolshoi
no more rich tsars nailing hats to heads

of course there's the bad stuff
like no product choice and grey queues for sameness

only one newspaper cynically called *truth*
all that corruption: the dachas, the kick-backs

* * *

it's not that I care if they call me pro-commo
it's a wonderful theory destroyed by men

from each according to ability
to each according to need sounds fine to me

A world based on sharing is utopian
human nature is basically mean

we're grasping, competitive and we know
even the purest have their price

I do care however, if they call me a spy
though spook sounds more friendly if a bit spectral

but it's treachery, treason – the weight of those words…
tarring and feathering and locking away

we know from telly – we love the spy catchers
our hair-swinging, chisel-chinned enforcers

they'd die for their country and they love their jobs
defeating the menace – red yellow or black

* * *

but it's all got more complex

those glamorous spooks are now on the nose

CIA MI5 they do their own thing

creating havoc all over the world

then Assange, Manning, Snowden

expose them and governments who lie

spies spying on spies

this new brand of 'traitor' – cult-figures. Heroes

Katharine blames herself for everything. She is quite sure it is her reputation that attracted attention to me.

Sitting on the verandah at Greenmount for the evening drink with the stir of the sea breeze cooling the air, she listens while I tell her everything that has happened.

Her forehead gathers in grief and anxiety.

'Oh darling, I didn't want this to happen. I don't care what they do to me. But you and Dodie...'

I try to reassure her it must have been something that Petrov had said.

It must be that. If it had been you why haven't ASIO questioned you too?

ITEM #55

innocent

adj. 1. not guilty of crime or offence. not responsible or directly involved: *an innocent bystander* 2. free from moral wrong; not corrupted. 3. not intended to cause offence; harmless. 4. (innocent of) without experience or knowledge of: *a man innocent of war cruelties.* without; lacking. n. an innocent person.

ITEM #56

Nationalism

These days, nationalism is a dirty word, redolent of the Australian flag, face paint and *Onya Straya Oi Oi Oi*. It is now completely synonymous with xenophobia. But that's chauvinism. Dad's brand of love for your country was not aggressive or racist. It had nothing to do with the flag. On the contrary, it was about escaping the early years of profound cultural cringe. A refusal to kowtow to Mother England and, later, Uncle Sam – to recognise the beauty of the bush, the vibrancy of our young democracy and the excellence and energy of our art and literature, especially our literature.

When we were kids, we were not allowed to read *Peter Rabbit, Milly Molly Mandy*, and especially Enid Blyton, who apparently bragged about churning out a book in a day. 'Yes, you can tell,' fumed dad, and 'imagine bragging about it.' So we were brought up on *The Magic Pudding, Blinky Bill* and *The Way of the Whirlwind*. When I wailed about wanting to read *The Magic Faraway Tree* like everyone else, dad explained how important it was to support our tiny literary tradition so it wasn't swamped by 'products from the dying Empire.'

Although we lived in suburban Canberra, we were one block away from the bush – Mount Ainslie, where I spent most of my childhood. Dad loved the bush. One of those random events that stay with you was the day we were walking through a stunning spotted gum forest. I remember him saying how important it was to treasure the bush, to watch it and learn from it. Spotted gums were particularly rewarding for this, with their ever changing foliage – their apricot bark, which peeled off to reveal bright green spots.

Dad also stressed the need to care for the bush, always. I was perplexed at the time, thinking at 13 that, of course, the bush cares for itself. But, along with Judith Wright, dad was a very early environmentalist – before we even knew the term.

Dad's horror of cultural cringe became even greater when even his own daughter appeared to be swept up in the US invention of 'teenagers', with all the attendant merchandising. He wrote a play expressing this horror: *Dr. Homer speaks: Oh Ailartsua Farewell*. This was a sort of pied piper story about Uncle Sam wooing away the youth of Australia with proms, jeans and the Mickey Mouse Club. The play was later televised by the ABC, a very exciting event for the family, even though I didn't recognise the message at the time.

Mind you, the first 'grown up' books dad gave me to read were *The Grapes of Wrath* and John Dos Passos's *U.S.A.* When I set off to explore the world, like many young Australians, I said in my callous, youthful way: 'I might be back if I don't find somewhere better to live.' Dad answered in his knowing, fatherly way: 'You won't.'

He was right. His brand of nationalism had rubbed off on me.

Broadly I would call Ric a 'socialist-liberal-internationalist', with the added fact that he is a convinced 'Australian nationalist' in all cultural matters...

Most of us are of course glad when we turn for home and get the smell of the homestead with the wind in our faces. Ric Throssell was more enthusiastic than anyone else I have known abroad in the service...

Partly this is for family reasons... But partly I am convinced this unusually strong nationalism is responsible – it is not directly political of course. Perhaps more of us could do with a dose of it.

PETER HEYDON

> 355. THE CHAIRMAN.—Mr. Throssell, you have told us that you are not a Communist. Would it be correct to say that you are not pro-Russian in outlook?—I do not think I am any more pro-Russian than I am pro-anything else.
>
> 356. PHILP, J.—But I take it you are more pro-Australian than you are pro-Russian?—Yes.

The evening newspapers which carry our faces smiling in relief that it is all over, blaze with the claim that I am pro-Russian, that Dodie allowed her party membership to lapse only after she joins the secret records branch of a government department in 1945.

Both statements are false and the opposite of what was said in the Commission.

ITEM #57

Each time the press misreport the evidence I ask my lawyer to bring it to the Commission's notice. The judges seem unconcerned. They blandly agree with the corrections and then explain there is nothing they can do about it.

Only the ABC corrects its report.

ITEM #58

As usual, *The Canberra Times* was a beacon of hope in the interests of honest reporting in the midst of a sea of dishonest, incompetent and sensationalised media. Norman Abjorensen writes, in 'A victim of intelligence game':

> The vendetta against now-retired diplomat Ric Throssell is a sad reflection on our reputation for fairness...
>
> Given the amount of attention devoted to Prichard and Throssell it is revealing to what extent the spooks were spooked by the Communist writer. But then, in Cold War Australia, the pen was seen as mighty indeed, accounting for the surveillance of many authors, among them Eleanor Dark, Mary Gilmore, Dymphna Cusack, Xavier Herbert, Rex Ingamells, Judah Waten, Allan Marshall, Cyril Pearl, Colin Simpson, Kenneth Slessor, Dal Stivens, Kylie Tenant and Bill Wannon.

Abjorensen quotes dad in an interview, surmising that the whole exercise was probably designed to 'get' Evatt and the Labor Party:

> 'There's always been this suggestion that Evatt...was somehow involved with my appointment to Moscow... I mean at the time Evatt was not only External Affairs minister but also Attorney-General as well as President of the General Assembly of the United Nations.'
>
> 'Why would he bother, let alone even know about the posting of a very junior diplomat?'

Abjorensen adds:

> Whatever it was, Throssell himself was 'got' at in a vendetta lasting almost his entire career.

The article exposes the particular attention of 'his apparent nemesis' Ron Richards, by then Deputy Director General of ASIO but formerly a WA police detective. Richards was 'notable for having stitched up a harmless group of crackpots during the war and having them and the Australia First members interned for plotting to communicate with the Japanese...'

While he illustrates Richards' 'dogged pursuit' on the one hand, he also exposes the constant snide undermining that occurred at the highest levels:

> Despite the rejection of allegations against Throssell, his departmental Secretary Arthur (later Sir Arthur) Tange wrote, presumably at ASIO's instigation, to the Commonwealth Solicitor-General, asking whether there were grounds for having Throssell and another person, charged under the Public Service Act.

'No charge against Mr. Throssell could possibly succeed,' was the reply, reiterating the main points from the Royal Commission's Report. Abjorensen points out the deliberate ambiguity in the rest of the letter, quoting it directly:

> 'From these matters it could be inferred that, for the present at any rate, Mr. Throssell's appointment to anything like a sensitive post in the career foreign service of Australia would be an embarrassment to his department... On another view, however, the whole affair may appear so vague and insubstantial that it should not be allowed to interfere at all with the officer's chosen career.'

Nudge, wink.

Abjorensen concludes:

> That a man such as Throssell should have had to withstand such outrageous treatment for so long for no reasons other than unconfirmed suspicion and association is a sad reflection on our reputation for fairness, and a blatant denial of natural justice.
>
> If the price of liberty is indeed eternal vigilance, the salutary lesson here is surely about proper vigilance and appropriate accountability of those who watch.

ITEM #59

Sport

Ric Arching

Other kids went to the footy with their dads, or played cricket in the backyard, or sat by the telly watching tennis all summer. When I was young and wanted to be like everyone else, I was jealous. The only thing dad did on weekends was escape to his shack and write, or go off 'to rehearsals.'

So we kids grew up fairly oblivious to Australia's great sporting claim to fame. The only sports we went in for were solitary ones like surfing (my brother and I) and horse riding (my sister).

Like his dad, or because of his influence, dad had been a good boxer, apparently a school champion at Wesley. There was even a big dinted silver (or not) trophy at Greenmount. Dad taught my brother Jim to box, after he had been bullied at school. When, as a stroppy young feminist, I accused dad of chauvinism, he taught me too. I still remember not to tuck my thumb in.

But dad's only real sporting interests were Shakespeare-related – fencing and archery. When his play *The Day Before Tomorrow* was chosen to be performed for the athletes at the Olympic Village in Melbourne in 1956, the whole family was given free tickets to all events. My sporty friends are still horrified to hear that the only ones mum and dad went to were fencing and archery! I was more interested in the wonderful new indoor phenomenon that hadn't yet arrived in Canberra – television!

While mum and dad were at the fencing, I was dressed up in my party dress watching *Rin Tin Tin* on a neighbour's new TV.

ITEM #60

The rest of Ric's life was like balancing on a see-saw. At one end was democracy: due process, 'innocent until proven guilty', even innocent when proven innocent. On the other: the continual insinuations by ASIO and their agents in the media, a political system incapable of defending principles it was meant to uphold, and the Public Service Promotions Board in league with the others.

After his gruelling week of 'trial by media' at the Royal Commission, Ric decided to test the assertion that his appearance at, and acquittal by, the Royal Commission should not affect his career in the public service:

A round of promotions is due… Is it really true that I will have the protection of the Public Service tribunals as the Commissioners suggest?

> **I decide I cannot let any reflection on my integrity go by – and apply...**

Junior colleagues are promoted over dad's head. He appeals and is told it has nothing to do with security, that the junior officers (with years' less experience) are chosen on the basis of 'efficiency'.

Within a few months, another group of young men are promoted above him.

Again he appeals.

Again he loses.

ITEM #61

Tables

At our home in Canberra, we had two tables full of stories – writing stories.

One was a burnished jarrah table with burgundy glints in the right light; probably our most precious piece of furniture in a house where much of it was second-hand.

I remember it being polished before the special occasions when there were visitors or special family feasts. Only on these rare occasions did we eat there and not at the kitchen table.

It was not only special because it was so beautiful. It was special because it was paid for with dad's first 'decent' royalty cheque. It was for *My Father's Son* – shortlisted for the prestigious Banjo Award.

Dad said he wasn't going to put his royalty money in the bank, or use it to pay ordinary household bills. He said he wanted to see something tangible for all that slog – something beautiful as well as useful.

The other table – another solid Australian hardwood, but decidedly scruffier – had originally been Katharine's kitchen table in Greenmount. According to family legend, dad was born on this table. Even as a kid, I was sceptical. OK, they were in the bush, so not near a hospital, and they didn't have much money, but they did have beds. Why not the bed? Having given birth myself, imagining giving birth on such an unforgiving surface, added to my scepticism.

Whether or not the birth story was dad using creative licence, the table came to Canberra after Katharine died. It became his writing desk – ensconced in his shack on our quarter-acre block. Apart from filing cabinets and his stern straight-backed chair, the desk was the only piece of furniture in the room. He probably spent more time sitting scribbling at that table than with us.

He would repair there for hours each weekend, having the odd break to chop wood for the 'Wonderheat' or to tend the veggie patch. Then, for the two weeks of the year when other families went to Coolangatta or Mossy Point for holidays, he would relish having a 'proper slab of writing time.' I didn't understand then.

When I was studying for my Leaving Certificate, dad announced with great ceremony that I could study at his desk in the evenings. (He must have been between books.) It was quite awesome, sitting at that seemingly huge desk, the whole room conducive to intense concentration. The high window looked onto the neighbour's straggling buddleia, which scraped against it companionably; the bare globe dangled on a cord, creating a compact circle on the table's battered surface. As my thoughts occasionally strayed from the causes of the Rum Rebellion or the subjunctive tense of the verb 'to know', I'd think, even if dad hadn't been born on that table, so many of his books had, and that was almost as special.

ITEM #62

Politics

Dad was never a political being in the way his mother was. Politics, in the form of deep ideological commitment, formed the core not only of Katharine's writing, but of her very being.

Dad was never interested in party politics or ideology as such. His last major work, *Tomorrow*, reflects this: he imagines the disillusionment of his characters with the models so fiercely defended by Katharine. When I was studying politics, first at ANU and then Adelaide University, my politics were much more like my grandmother's. Dad and I would have frequent arguments about ideology, especially in relation to the role of imperialism and capitalism in undermining the economies of third-world countries.

I remember one particularly ferocious argument. I asserted that all overseas economic aid was reactionary because it merely propped up inequality and stifled the development of local political alternatives to capitalism. I had forgotten about dad's pivotal work with the Colombo Plan, which primarily used training as aid to developing countries, and his time as the Head of the International Training Branch of External Affairs – a project about which he was both passionate and proud. His colleague from that time, Greg O'Reardon, spoke at dad's funeral and praised his distinguished contribution to Australia's foreign aid program, and the fact that he converted a minor extension of Australia's foreign policy into Australia's most extensive, concrete and beneficial international relations program ever.

Students yell at Mr Rusk

University students hoisted a Vietcong flag and yelled abuse at the United States Secretary of State, Mr Rusk, at the official opening of the SEATO Council at the Canberra Theatre Centre yesterday.

Waving a home-made version of the red and blue Vietcong flag, about 40 members of the Vietnam Action Committee picketed the theatre throughout the ceremony.

As the delegates left the theatre, the students gathered opposite the waiting official cars, facing a strong police guard.

A girl university student, who said later she wanted Mr Rusk to have a closer look at her placard, was grabbed and pushed off the roadway by ACT police when she tried to run up to his car.

Her placard was torn up and she was warned by the police. She would not give her name to reporters.

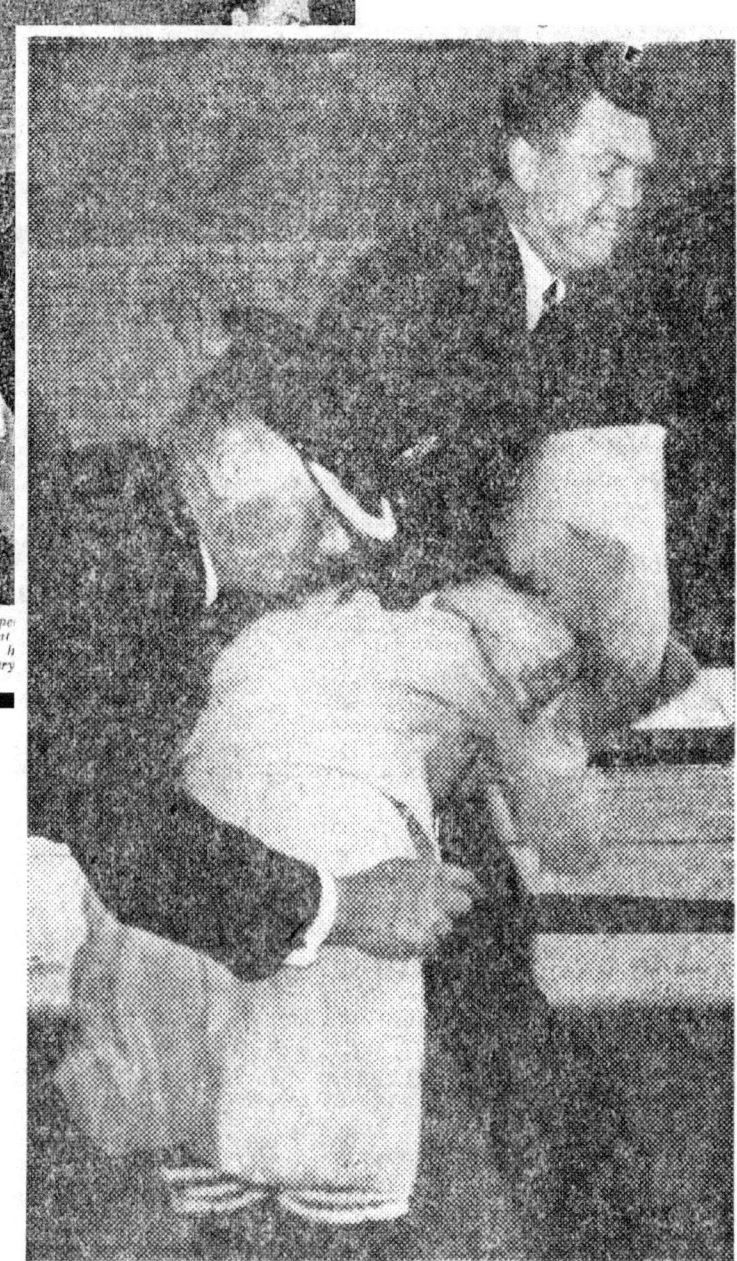

Members of the Vietnam Action Committee hold up the Vietcong flag as SEATO delegates arrive.

Inspe
Kent
she h
retary

However, like his mother, he had a huge commitment to social justice and to the peace movement in particular. He believed that we are here on this earth to make a difference. And he also felt that he was best placed to do this through his writing.

While not being a pacifist – he always said he'd kill in defence of his loved ones, and he did serve as a soldier in the Second World War – he was a staunch activist and campaigner for the peace movement. Many of his plays espoused this theme: *For Valour* was based on the life of his father; *Valley of the Shadows* was about the hysterical blindness of an Australian soldier as a symbol of the world closing its eyes to the drift towards war; and *Legend* was a Cold War love story with an anti-war message.

Dad was a long-term member of both the People for Nuclear Disarmament and Writers against Nuclear Arms. At his funeral, fellow members paid glowing tribute not only to his ready willingness to give talks at a wide range of venues (from schools to the Australian Defence Academy), but also to his use of his considerable diplomatic skills in fundraising and negotiation. They were particularly impressed by his willingness to get his hands dirty – trooping tirelessly around to bookshops and libraries, quite unlike those who don't like to be out of the limelight.

Despite my very political grandmother and her huge influence on me, like many of my generation, I was truly politicised by the Vietnam War.

I went to my first anti-Vietnam War protest when I was still in high school. It was a silent vigil outside parliament house, so it was pretty tame compared to the later heady years of the Vietnam Moratoria. But when I agreed to stand there by candlelight for four hours, I forgot that I was on crutches! I'd broken a bone in my foot (running down some wet stairs in thongs) but had become so used to the crutches that I began to think they were the normal way to get around. I was applauded by the organisers for my 'courage and commitment', but I felt that I, unlike everyone else, had something to prop myself up with.

When I started at ANU in 1966, my majors were initially English, History and IPL (introduction to philosophy and logic). This changed, however, after a bruising episode with the English Department. An 'excellent essay mark' was challenged by the head of department because 'your father probably wrote it.' Dad hadn't even read Jane Austen – let alone had any interest in writing my essay on Austen and feminism for me. This, coinciding with the *realpolitik* of the Vietnam War, meant that I was ripe for a transfer to the Politics Department. It was a vibrant, active and very left-wing department, headed up by the indomitable Finn Crisp and including staff like Bruce McFarlane – a brilliant and eccentric radical who became my friend and mentor.

As ASIO implies in relation to dad and his mother, I must have had politics in my blood. I took to it like a duck to water. I was very lucky studying Australian politics and International Relations at a time so turbulent and exciting for both Australia and South East Asia; this enabled me to marry theory and practice in a way that might have been less possible in other eras.

From that time, my major passion was politics. Although I enjoyed history, I could not cope with the Logic side of IPL – too mathematical. (Maybe I wasn't ever that logical.) I studied Politics for three years – adding an extra honours year with Bruce where I studied Marxist theory. Just like Katharine, I was blown away by Marx's prescience in so many ways. And I was terribly sad that I discovered him after she had died. I so longed to tell her that I was no longer an individualist!

In my first year, I joined the tiny ANU Vietnam Action Committee, many of whose members have become famous for different political reasons over the years. At our first demonstration, all 12 or so of us marched around and around Garema Place in Canberra, to show the Friday night shoppers the true evil of US imperialism. The Canberra police considered us important enough to deserve a heavy presence but didn't make a move when some of the local thugs started hitting and kicking us as we trooped by. It was a very educational experience.

History shows that 'from little things big things grow.' The numbers at these demonstrations grew and grew throughout Australia, culminating in the 100,000 strong Vietnam Moratoria.

The ANU group travelled to both Sydney and Melbourne to join these huge protests. As a long-term claustrophobe, I found them completely overwhelming: wonderful, in this enormous number of people from all walks of life coming together to fight injustice, but terrifying, in the sheer mass of humanity all pressed together. I remember that the crush in Sydney was so tight, my feet no longer touched the ground; I was carried forward by the mass of bodies. I felt as if I was swimming, pushing through with my arms, duck paddling underneath.

In Canberra, the protests grew and grew, both in size and audacity. When US Secretary of State Dean Rusk came to Canberra, we planned big demos that would attract the press – who were getting tired of filming people standing around with placards, chanting *Hey Hey LBJ how many bombs have you dropped today*. A few of us (all young women, strangely) were delegated to stand at the front of the crowd and then 'storm onto the road' just before the procession of black limos crawled by. Unfortunately, I was the only bunny who did it!

Next morning's *Canberra Times* had a front-page photo of me being tackled by a huge plainclothes copper. All you can see of me is my 'witches' britches'. These were basically fancy long-johns to keep out the Canberra winter – knee length and black, with layers of lace to distinguish them from the old man sort.

A friend who was a cadet journalist on the paper at the time found a reference to me in a file, identifying me 'as the one who rushed Dean Rusk's car.'

I also did a one-night stint in gaol after a sit down protest against the gaoling of one of our first conscientious objectors – Simon Townsend. It was an incredibly memorable night, not just because there were 18 of us in a cell meant for 6, but because one of our number was Jeannie Lewis – a wonderful folk singer who sang for us and with us, for most of the night... One thing about gaol cells – the acoustics are wonderful.

My youthful enthusiasm for the cause was worrying dad, not because he didn't support me – he strongly opposed Australia's support for US involvement in local Vietnamese politics – but because he thought I wasn't nearly cautious enough...

I remember, after a long phone conversation to a fellow activist about the campaign, dad took me aside and warned me to be much more careful about what I said over the phone. *Of course our phone is tapped. They've always been interested in us...*

But when Gough Whitlam got into power and one of the first things he did was to withdraw our troops from Vietnam, we all stopped being activists and got on with our studies and careers. I did my year's teaching in a country town called Crookwell – famous for fat lambs and spuds – and then went on the traditional young Australian's overseas odyssey for a couple of years.

ITEM #63

702. LIGERTWOOD, J.—There is no such evidence.

703. PHILP, J.—Dr. Louat, we have no direct concern with the effect on his career. In this regard, if his career was affected, he would have his rights of appeal at law to the tribunal in the Public Service, where no doubt only legal evidence would be admissible.

704. DR. LOUAT.—That may well be.

705. PHILP, J.—You are suggesting that his superiors may act upon the evidence before us, or upon anything we say? You are assuming that?

706. DR. LOUAT.—Yes.

707. PHILP, J.—I think that is a wrong assumption.

708. DR. LOUAT.—I have a worse apprehension than that. I think they may be perhaps disposed to act on their view of the total material that has been reported—not only the officers themselves, but those who are in contact in one way or the other.

709. PHILP, J.—But Mr. Throssell would have the protection of the law, Doctor.

justice n.

1. just behaviour or treatment. the quality of being just. 2. the administration of the law or authority in maintaining this.

ITEM #64

Phillip Deery (academic expert on ASIO and the Cold War)

In an article in *Overland* in 2011, Deery cites several examples of other innocent men (the carpenter, the scientist and the doctor) whose careers were stymied and lives ruined by ASIO victimisation because of minor acts of political dissent, like attending a union or a protest meeting. While even these small examples of political dissent could not be ascribed to my father, the one thing they had in common was that the nature of their employment in combination with this dissent (or, in dad's case, his mother's dissent) was seen as sufficient grounds to declare them a security risk.

> But none was in fact a security threat or remotely associated with any espionage that could have justified ASIO's compilation of dossiers, reliance on informants and job vetting.

ITEM #65

The *Royal Commission on Espionage Act* forbade an employer to take any action against an employee because he or she had been called as a witness.

I have been acting head of the section and hope that enough time has passed for the mud that has been thrown at me to be forgotten.

Perhaps this time I will make the step to First Secretary. I had been in the Department thirteen years and it was seven years since I had been made a Second Secretary.

A man junior to me who had never worked in the UN Branch is promoted to the position I have been in so long.

It seems like a personal affront.

ITEM #66

Once again, he appeals to the First Secretary.

Once again, his appeal is rejected.

He then appeals to the Public Service Board, arguing that his refusal to enquire into the political beliefs of personal friends is not an adequate reason to deny him promotion.

Point by point I trace the history of the case.

I write a detailed nine page statement for the Promotions Appeal Committee in good public service style. A copy goes off to the Secretary.

It makes no difference.

Deep in his heart, dad knew that appeals to those who had already made up their minds were useless, but there was nothing else he could do. He had to continue to protest until somebody heard. He tried again.

Of course, he was sure he had lost. Then he received a phone call:

> You don't know me. I was the association rep on your last appeal.
>
> I shouldn't be telling you this, d'you know what I mean?
>
> You won that appeal for the EAO Grade 3. I thought you ought to know, that's all.
>
> It's bloody disgraceful what the department is doing to you, d'you know what I mean?

Dad was elated. He could hardly believe it. It seemed too good to be true.

And it was. A month later, he was told he had lost the appeal.

> It is worse when I expect I am going to win. As if all delusions have been torn away, I can see there is no future for me in External Affairs. I have to get out, escape – somewhere, anywhere...

ITEM #67

Frank Wheeler

Dear Sir Arthur

You will recall our discussion at home one night regarding the recent aspects of one of your continuing problems. You will recall also that I raised the question of **'an innocuous promotion'**. I should be glad to know whether you have any further thoughts after checking on the matter. In the meantime, we are continuing to keep the current report of the Promotions Appeal committee in the 'ice-box'.

Yours sincerely, FH Wheeler, Chairman

ITEM #68

Promotion! Head of the Training and Welfare section of the Economic and Technical Assistance Branch!

It seems like deliverance. EAO Grade 3. And I feel as though I am king.

Dad stays in the position for 13 years, after which he decides to try again to work in the department where his skills and interests really lie. But his hopes for a return to External Affairs are dashed in the same old way. When he insists that he be told why (after all, they couldn't go on pretending, after all this time), he is told 'security considerations' prevented his assignment to other areas of Foreign Affairs.

I have to accept I have to go on living with suspicion for the rest of my life.

When I face up to it I know I have been crippled.

They keep on telling you, you aren't good enough – it becomes true.

ITEM #69

the man who wasn't there

he was there again today,

parking darkly discreetly distanced,

disappearing fast around sharp corners,

stepping behind me, stopping

when I turn

why are they watching?

what have I done?

they all seem to know,

eyes averted, stage whispers halting

when I pass

Ric Throssell, under a portrait of his political activist mother, Katherine Susannah Prichard, in his Canberra home.

discreet parking, snide whispers,

disappearing around corners,

stop!

I say,

what have I done?

you know what you've done, confess!

the red queen shouts,

off with his head!

black crows line up in judgement,

you're FAARked...

confess they squark,
what have I done?
how can I confess when I have no idea?

ah so you've committed the crime
of not knowing your crime

off with his head!
so the crime of innocence?
don't get smart, you know what you've done,
but you just said I didn't,
you're FAARrked scream the crows

the judges roar,

shrieks and cackles, mad barnyard laughter,

undercurrent of crow,

you'll never escape us – we know what you've done,

I'm screaming now – **what have I done?**

you've got *us* for life and then it's

your kids, guilty forever of 'not knowing your crime'

 so they have it all too – mindless blather from the Fourth Estate,

meaningless questions from donkeys in suits

off with their heads!

so you're bad cos you're wrong and

you're wrong cos you're bad?

and the children cry: *what did he do?*

guilty as charged.

ITEM #70

Punishment

Dad was passionately opposed to corporal punishment.

I went to school in the days when you could still get 'the cuts' if you were a boy. I don't remember girls ever getting caned by the headmaster, but hit with a ruler by the teacher, yes.

When I got smacked over the knuckles by my sewing teacher for making my feather stitch sampler 'all grubby', I made the mistake of showing my swollen hands to dad. The next day, he stormed to school in a fury, and you could hear his voice from the headmaster's office. Dad was terrifying when he was angry. He didn't need to smack us!

Our usual punishment for naughtiness was 'time-out' in the bathroom (too many books in our bedroom). But he also had his version of making the punishment fit the crime.

Once, when I was about seven or eight, a few of us neighbourhood kids were convinced by our local bad lad to check out what he claimed was an abandoned house. When we climbed in through the window, it clearly wasn't abandoned – even down to food still on the table. To our horror, he started nicking things and stuffing them in his pockets. When we mortified kids tried to make a quick exit, he barred the door. He threated to bash us if we didn't take something, so that they couldn't only blame one person.

To my shame, we complied, and I grabbed a block of butter from the plate on the table.

When the police came around to our house, I confessed and produced the butter from my bedroom drawer. My shocked father insisted on the following punishment: I was to buy a new block of butter with my pocket money and then sit the stolen slab on a plate in front of my place at the table, for my exclusive use, until it was finished – a daily reminder of my crime. It seemed to take months.

Worst of all, I had to take the new butter to the family and apologise. They were very kind about it – even laughed, saying they knew it was all the work of 'that bad lad.'

But I went right off butter. That slab sitting there is branded in my memory.

ITEM #71

Although he had never been a member of the ALP, let alone the Communist Party, dad was elated when Gough Whitlam came to power in 1972 after 23 years of Liberal government. Like many people, he felt excited at the mere prospect of change. He also had more specific reasons to celebrate, although he tried not to have any expectations.

I refuse to allow myself to think that the change will make any difference to me, but there is the promise of a security review tribunal, which Gough talked about in that first campaign speech.

ITEM #72

Dad was always very principled about not using contacts or asking friends for help, and his ego was so battered that he was terribly afraid of refusal. But he dared to feel a bit optimistic after Gough Whitlam's first hundred days.

Someone as firmly committed to reform, redressing injustice – this might be different...

It wasn't. At the time, Gough didn't seem interested (although his then secretary, Peter Wilenski, later told dad that *the correction of that old injustice* was something Gough regretted being unable to address because of his untimely removal). But the new, iconoclastic Attorney-General – Lionel Murphy – was interested. I can remember the excitement in our house after a 2am phone call. Murphy was at a party, had just found out about 'this terrible injustice' and was going to get to the bottom of it. Dad allowed himself to be hopeful again. If anyone could challenge those ASIO boys, Lionel could. Was it really possible that my father might at last be freed of those unwarranted suspicions?

But while he waited for something to eventuate from this early promise, the Labor government was unceremoniously dismissed.

Despite this dashing of his larger hopes, dad was buoyed in the short term, because Labor's brief spell in office did seem to afford him some more friends in power. Alan Renouf, who had become Secretary of the Department of Foreign Affairs, had been a colleague since they were first diplomatic cadets together. Renouf was finally able to exert sufficient influence to have security clearance lifted to allow a promotion to level 1 within the Aid Agency (a position in which he had worked for more than 10 years). Later, he was to approve dad's return to the Department of Foreign Affairs in charge of International Cultural Relations.

> **Culture is at the bottom of the barrel as far as foreign policy is concerned. Whenever there were cuts to be made, culture was the first cut.**

Dad knew little about the international visual arts scene and berated himself for it. However, his interest in, and knowledge of, the literary and theatre worlds made the job more rewarding than it might have been. Unfortunately, given his fervent desire to be acknowledged in the 'real work' of the department, the worst irony was to come.

ITEM #73

When he thought that three years in Cultural Relations had served as a *bureaucratic absolution for my presumed sins,* dad dared once more to stick his head up above the parapet and apply for yet another job he had been acting in – 11 times, he counted.

This time, he was told that, even if he had been able to obtain a higher security clearance, his chance of success was hampered by the 20 years in which he did not have overseas and management experience.

He replied, in his own defence, that it was like chopping someone's legs off and then penalising them because they couldn't run.

ITEM #74

When the evidence doesn't fit the (foregone) conclusion

710. DR. LOUAT.—I appreciate what Your Honours are putting. I know Your Honours cannot do or say more than is within Your Honours' function. That is why I am not pressing Your Honours. I am not asking Your Honours to say what it is not within your scope to say. I only say that this will no doubt be one of the matters with which you will deal in your final report, and that everyone ought to suspend his judgment until that time.

711. THE CHAIRMAN.—I would imagine that that probably would be the case, Dr. Louat. However, that is only my supposition.

712. DR. LOUAT.—Yes. But I take it that Your Honour Mr. Justice Philp and Your Honour Mr. Justice Ligertwood would have the same expectation?

713. LIGERTWOOD, J.—Dr. Louat—I am not speaking for my colleagues—I do not mind saying that there is no evidence of any impropriety against Mr. Throssell. There has been before us none that I have seen.

714. DR. LOUAT.—I thank Your Honour.

An obvious injustice – Throssell clearly a scapegoat
We were not impressed with his deportment
Witnesses were promised they wouldn't be punished
A loyal subject, not a security risk

We were not impressed with his deportment
It would be wrong to hold he was a Klod member
A loyal subject, not a security risk
Not known to be a spy, but suspicion is strong

It would be wrong to hold he was a Klod member
We couldn't prove he was communist
Not known to be a spy, but suspicion is strong
No evidence of any impropriety

We couldn't prove he was communist
No reason to bar him from classified information
No evidence of any impropriety
No reasonable doubt he was one time a spy

No reason to bar him from classified information
Venona is partial – his innocence is possible
No reasonable doubt he was one time a spy
Petrov's evidence –remote hearsay and assertion

Venona is partial – his innocence is possible
Witnesses were promised they wouldn't be punished
Petrov's evidence –remote hearsay and assertion
Throssell clearly a scapegoat. An obvious injustice.

ITEM #75

irony

n. (pl. -ies) the expression of meaning through the use of language signifying the opposite, typically for humorous effect. a state of affairs that appears perversely contrary to what one expects. (also dramatic or tragic irony). a literary technique originally used in Greek tragedy, by which the significance of a character's words or actions are clear to the audience or reader, although unknown to the character.

ITEM #76

But they're always so smart on the telly

CODES:

LM..........Les Murray (conservative Australian poet)

KHT........Karen Han Throssell

EMJ........Ethel May Jordan (my maternal grandmother)

KSP.........Katharine Susannah Prichard (my paternal grandmother)

FERRO...ASIO's code name for Ric Throssell

CPA........Communist Party of Australia

PA...........Phillip Adams (radio journalist and broadcaster)

LM called us 'trendy lefties'
back then on the barricades.
But we really *did* care.
We joked that you had to pass
a stupidity test
to get into ASIO.

They try to mingle incognito
with their neatly clipped beards,
string of hippie beads
and shiny black shoes.
We sneak around them
taking their photos.

As transcript in our file
finding evidence for their truth
they quote KHT at length
on the doings of her gran (KSP)
Important source, vital information.
She was four, and was referring to EMJ (the other gran)

CODES:

LM..........Les Murray (conservative Australian poet)

KHT........Karen Han Throssell

EMJ........Ethel May Jordan (my maternal grandmother)

KSP.........Katharine Susannah Prichard (my paternal grandmother)

FERRO...ASIO's code name for Ric Throssell

CPA........Communist Party of Australia

PA...........Phillip Adams (radio journalist and broadcaster)

In the same file, they failed to get

the famous spy's name right –

the man with the mother.

His name was not Richard,

nor Pritchard, nor Throssel (with one 'l')

And it was never Ferro.

And earlier, when our democracy

was trying to ban the CPA,

they raided KSP's home

looking for subversive material.

Aha! they cried, scuttling off with

schoolboy notes on the Peasant Revolt.

PA finds in his file mention of

his membership of the 'Slatterst' society.

ASIO was puzzled. They searched.

Did they meet in rooms darkened by Venetian blinds?

Were they slovenly in demeanour and appearance?

Years later a cautious entry with a query – 'Flat Earth Society'?

ITEM #77

Notwithstanding what Aarons calls the widespread 'mythology' of the Left that these allegations of espionage were all part of a conspiracy to destroy them, he shows that espionage was organised from the early 1940s by Wally Clayton...and that its major source was agents in the Department of External Affairs. So, despite what he describes as 'many stupidities, considerable crudeness and frequent lapses of professionalism, ASIO had a legitimate task' and **'stands in contrast to intelligence services in communist countries, which established elaborate networks to intimidate their own citizens and compiled dossiers on millions of innocent people.'**

ITEM #78

Well I don't know [my friend says], either you've been very hard done by or you're some kind of Philby or Blunt.

Of course! They think I am some kind of plant like Burgess and McLean. Everything I do is a cover for something else.

Everything I say is a front. All everyday things are subterfuge.

ITEM #79

Both services would have done much less damage to their countries, moral and financial, if they had simply been disbanded.

JOHN LE CARRÉ, WRITING IN 1991 ON THE COLD WAR
INTELLIGENCE SERVICES OF THE US AND THE UK

ITEM #80

In 1978, dad was finally offered a job that, he felt, offered some acknowledgement of his years of experience. The directorship of the Commonwealth Foundation was an appointment with some public kudos.

Something that will let me see out my last few years before retirement, feeling I have got somewhere and done something useful with my life.

ITEM #81

falsify

v. (-ies,-ied) 1. alter (information or evidence) so as to mislead 2. prove (statement or theory) to be false.

ITEM #82

My brother Jim Throssell speaks

Hello Jess [old family friend]

I'm sorry I didn't see you on my last visit to Canberra.

I did want to thank you for your concern over Des Ball's scurrilous article defaming my folks.

Through the 40 years I spent with them, our relationship evolved to discussing everything and anything, whether we were proud of it or not. If they had been guilty as accused, I'm sure that by the end, they would have had their reasons, and would have told me. Instead, all I ever saw was struggle and anguish over the wrong done to them, and the damage to their reputation.

One of the last things Ric said to me on the topic was 'When I'm dead, the cowards will come out of the shadows, because I won't be around to defend myself against their libel. Don't waste your energy fighting them; you'll have even less chance than I did. At least you might know who they are.'

And a decade after their death, out slinks Des Ball.

Sadly, I still lost sleep over his nasty article. If he were in the scientific community, his methods and lack of consistency would be ridiculed. The self-appointed spy-catcher who thinks he can out-sniff 50 years of ASIO agents. He and his likes were not so bold when Ric & Dodie were around to respond with a libel suit.

Enough of this.

Thank you for your faith, and concern. I'm touched, and I'm sure they would be flattered. They always held you and Bert in such high regard. To the Throssell kids, you were always Auntie Jess.

Warmest wishes, Jim (February 2012)

BREAKING
THE CODES

ITEM #83

The release of the Venona decrypts also leads to the emergence of another (apparently unlikely) Cold War warrior – Des Ball. I had known him at the ANU in the 60s as an anti-Vietnam War comrade, but dad later knew him as his new nemesis after the publication of Ball's book, *Breaking the Codes,* co-authored with David Horner.

ITEM #84

Breaking the codes – review by Phil Deery

In his review, Phil Deery comments on the amount of publicity generated by the release of the book in 1998:

> Both the *SMH* and *The Australian* ran front-page feature articles captioned 'the Moscow connection' and reviews of the book appeared in all the major newspapers.

While he understood that reviewers were invariably generous in their praise of Ball and Horner's assiduous research, because it added significantly to our knowledge of the role and influence of counterespionage and signals intelligence (a 'missing dimension' in Cold War literature), he does note that the book has several flaws, some serious:

> Ball and Horner, in my view, are insufficiently sceptical of their sources. Given the heavy dependence on ASIO files, a critical evaluation of the reliability and partiality of raw intelligence data seems essential. Instead we find tantalizing citations such as 'Documents held by ASIO' whose judgements are accepted without reservation. The Cold War, after all, produced mindsets at both ends of the ideological spectrum...

> [Ball and Horner] do an historical disservice to her son Ric Throssell... The Venona releases of October 1996 exonerated him. No other evidence that implicates him in espionage has emerged.

Nor does it in *Breaking the Codes.* Yet the authors deliberately leave the door open:

> At the least he was an 'unwitting'... member of the Klod group. At the worst 'according to some of the ASIO officers' most familiar with the case, he assisted the KGB... Neither of these accusations, made by others but accepted by the authors, is supported by source citation; **indeed, they epitomize the innuendo that has blighted Throssell's life.**

ITEM #85

Letter to the editor

(unpublished)

Submitted to *The Canberra Times* 10 September 1996

Jack Waterford is half right. His review of Des Ball and Dave Horner's history of the intelligence service in Australia (*Canberra Times* September 5th) finds little new in its 468 pages: fresh details of old facts, new allegations, few revelations.

He is quite correct. I am rankled. After 30 years being well and truly 'under the prism' I had thought their case against me more than 'far from convincing.' I had hoped it could be finally closed; but I dare say suspicion will never need more than suspicion itself to feed on.

And there is more to *Breaking the Codes* than that. There are too, unsubstantiated allegations presented as demonstrated fact; conclusions based upon unrelated events; quotations out of context as evidence of spurious assertions and evidence contrary to their hypotheses omitted and ignored.

I have no doubt that my mother, Katharine Susannah Prichard, boasted – 'gossiped' if you prefer Waterford's word, about my accomplishments real or imagined, to anyone who would listen.

On the basis of that, and her admitted admiration for the Soviet Union, her hospitality to the newly arrived *Tass* correspondents and her articles on Australian literature for the Soviet monthly *International Literature*, she is accused by Ball and Horner of treachery and spying, 50 years after the event!

It may be that Ball and Horner can make any unsubstantiated accusations they want against those who are dead and beyond legal defamation. But is it also beyond the law that the beliefs of unidentified ASIO officers as to my witting involvements in espionage should be published by those regarded by some reputable academics as no more than incompetent stooges of ASIO?

Ric Throssell

ITEM #86

Breaking the Codes produces some useful information

While rehashing only the same old allegations and assertions about my father, the book did explore the wider political implications and the really important players in this saga – the role of MI5 in setting the agenda for Australian policy during the Cold War:

> The spy case brought in several of the world's most secret intelligence organisations; intensified the suspicion that led to the Cold War; caused Australia to be cut off for two years from United States intelligence exchanges; led to the setting up of Australian Security Intelligence Organisation under British guidance; and helped entrench 23 years of conservative rule in Canberra.

They describe how, as the Cold War was intensifying in 1948 into a sharply defined confrontation overseas, Australia was still ambivalent. Evatt and his department head, John Burton, were still trying to improve relations with the Soviet Union and to practise 'open diplomacy'. Chifley also refused to follow the British response of banning communists from its public service.

Australia was regarded as unreliable in relation to security matters, so the US had been progressively reducing the amount of information they passed to us. In May 1948, the US authorities decided on a 'complete embargo on the transfer of classified US information to Australia.' This was only reversed in 1950, after Menzies had been elected Prime Minister.

The British push for greater security eventually succeeded when Chifley was persuaded to accept an MI5 proposal to replace the 'ineffective Commonwealth Investigation Service' with a new security organisation – the Australian Security and Intelligence Service (ASIS), with its own resident MI5 liaison officer.

ITEM #87

Key Petrov identity dies

A key figure in the 1954 Petrov spy inquiry, Mr Ric Throssell, has been found dead in his Canberra home.

Mr Throssell, the son of Gallipoli Victoria Cross winner Hugo Throssell and writer and communist activist Katharine Susannah Prichard, was named as a Soviet agent in April 1953 by Soviet defector Vladimir Petrov.

Although the allegations were later dismissed by the Petrov royal commission, Mr Throssell never succeeded in totally clearing his name and found his career in the then Department of External Affairs repeatedly blocked by ASIO.

The 1996 release of the Venona cables, the secret US intercepts of Soviet diplomatic cables, saw Mr Throssell again labelled a Soviet agent by a major newspaper, prompting him to take legal action.

The cables confirmed the Soviets had given him the code name Ferro, and were interested in him and his wife, Dorothy, a communist in her student days. But they gave no indication that the Throssells ever worked for the Soviet Union.

Mr Throssell claimed the cables as a vindication, but the 1998 book *Breaking the Codes* by Des Ball and David Horner concluded there was evidence that Mr Throssell had passed infor-

Ric Throssell

mation on to the Soviets and was regarded by them at least as a member of the so-called Klod group.

However, the book found it was unclear whether Mr Throssell was a Soviet agent or simply an unwitting source of information to his mother, who was a conduit to the Soviets.

Mr Throssell was found dead in his home following the death the same day of his wife, Dorothy, who had suffered a long illness. Police confirmed they were investigating the deaths in Canberra.

"Until such time as a suspicious death can be discounted, there's always an investigation," a police spokeswoman said.

But Mr Throssell's solicitor said there was no question of foul play.

A joint funeral will be held tomorrow.

AAP

witch-hunt

n. 1. an attempt to find and punish a particular group of people who are being blamed for something, often simply because of their opinions, not because they have actually done anything wrong.

2. a vigorous campaign to round up or expose dissenters on the pretext of safeguarding the welfare of the public.

ITEM #88

Cold War secrets and the spies who came out of Canberra

Gerard Henderson:

Last week the National Archives in Britain released new material about Vladimir and Evdokia Petrov…

The release of the MI5 files [tells us] that according to a top secret cable, Sir Charles Spry, the Director General of ASIO, advised that, in the event of the Labor leader, Bert Evatt, becoming Prime Minister after the 1954 election, the British government should withhold important secrets from Australia.

In *The Australian* last Monday, both [Robert] Manne and [David] McKnight [author of *Australian Spies and their Secrets*] criticised Spry's actions. Manne said that Spry had an allegiance to 'some concept of a broader free world, not to the elected Australian government'. McKnight described Spry's actions as 'disturbing' and 'a little scary'.

But was it? Spry knew then what we know now. Evatt was minister for external affairs from October 1941 to December 1949. During the second half of the 1940s Josef Stalin's Soviet Union infiltrated his department.

The USSR's chief agent in Australia was Wally Clayton and his spies in the Department of External Affairs included Ric Throssell (the son of the communist writer Katharine Susannah Prichard), Ian Milner, and Jim Hill.

ITEM #89

Letter to the editor

(unpublished)

Submitted to the *Sydney Morning Herald* 15 April 2011

Dear Sir,

As I read Gerard Henderson's article 'Cold War secrets and the spies who came out of Canberra' 12/04/11, I was shocked to read that even as a member of the paranoid right, he is able to agree with Colonel Spry that ASIO should subvert an elected Australian government. I thought *when are all these old Cold War warriors going to get it right?*

Gerard Henderson got one thing right – that when it comes to writing about the Cold War mentality of the 1950s 'that the theory is very much fiction.' But unfortunately he himself continues this fiction. In November 2010 I appealed to the Press Council to insist that *The Australian* print a correction to their (anonymous) assertions that the Throssell family were all Russian spies, and here is Gerard Henderson still at it.

The reason for [Throssell's] failure to get a security clearance...had nothing whatsoever to do with his loyalty, judgement or competence. Ric Throssell was a sacrificial pawn caught up unwittingly in intelligence work, Mr Alan Renouf, former Secretary of the Department of Foreign Affairs, has said.

Friends suggested that dad had good grounds to seek compensation after 30 years of denial of normal career advancement.

But it wasn't money dad wanted, it was justice. He spent most of his life trying to clear his name and redress this huge injustice against him and his family. It is most thoroughly documented in his book *My Father's Son* mentioned above. Ironically he had thought of naming it *The man who had a mother...*

Yours sincerely,

Karen Throssell

ITEM #90

The spy who came out as Klod

Desmond Ball wrote in The Australian in 2011 about Walter Seddon Clayton, whose code name was Klod. He was the spymaster who ran Australia's network of KGB spies from 1944 to 1950. Ball visited him and his wife Peace at their home on the coast northeast of Sydney in 1996. Ball wrote that:

> in addition to his admission to being Klod, and despite her [Peace's] guardianship [of the conversation] he did make three important points at times when she left the room.
>
> First, he strongly believed he had been the most 'powerful man' in the CPA... He had not only been 'in the centre of operations' in the party, but had been principally responsible for directing these operations.
>
> Second, he described some of the key aspects of the operational functioning of the spy network... But he cast new light on the role of Doris Isabel Beeby and the process by which he collected classified material **from his agents in the Department of External Affairs: [including] Dorothy Throssell (nee Jordan) (Podruga) in 1945-47, and Ric Throssell (Ferro) in 1945 and 1947-49...**
>
> Third, Clayton remained convinced that 'the socialist revolution will still happen.' He said that with the collapse of the Soviet Union in 1991 communists had lost 'the first round'. However, he enthusiastically awaited 'the next round', telling me about the next generation of covert communists and referring me to the children of those who had been in his spy network. He and Peace had been, I think, childless. But he made me wonder about which particular members of his Klod group he might have in mind. I have known several of their offspring, and cannot believe any of these would have served his agenda. In the end Clayton's 'next round' was simply the wishful thinking of a deluded old man.

ITEM #91

I can't quite believe it. Why do they need to keep this fairy story alive – after all these years? There wasn't even the *I, Spry* documentary to trigger this one.

This was an interview Des Ball conducted with Wally Clayton in 1996 – why trot it out now?

It would be very egocentric of me to imagine that it has appeared as an answer to my charge of 'where's the evidence?' – especially given his little swipe about the 'offspring'. Who but the people he's maligning and their relatives would care about all this now?

Very perplexing, but still deeply annoying – especially as I don't know how to *make it go away*!

Particularly because he claims to have interviewed the source of the allegations, and it is Wally Clayton himself.

Why would Wally Clayton dob in innocent people? Maybe because he didn't want to go down alone? Or maybe he was senile and forgot who was innocent and who was being inaccurately named by Petrov.

And even though Des Ball is an exemplary product of the Harvard training ground for CIA agents, he would still value his academic reputation too much to jeopardise it by inventing this story. Wouldn't he?

ITEM #92

Letter to the editor

(unpublished)

Submitted to *The Australian* 29 September 2011

As one of the 'offspring' of the alleged Russian spy ring, I am forced yet again to correct the continuing misinformation about my father, promulgated by Des Ball. ('The Spy who came out as Klod' 24/09/11.)

But at least *The Australian* is improving its sources, having moved on from an article by an anonymous ex-ASIO agent (November 2010) to yourself – Professor Des Ball of the Centre for Strategic Studies. The interesting thing is that you are now quoting Wally Clayton as the source of your 'evidence', saying that he named both my mother and father as his agents.

But *The Australian* is not being consistent. In 1996 when it ran a front-page photo linking my father Ric Throssell and the self-confessed spy Wally Clayton – the threat of a defamation suit forced it to apologise. In the apology, the paper stated that the Venona tapes had established that Throssell *was not part of a spy ring*.

And now you claim that Clayton says he was. Who is to be believed?

On the one side, we have an ancient and deluded ex-spy, for whom deception and intrigue were his modus operandi, and who was regarded by the Royal Commission as 'someone whose evidence could not be relied on.' On the other, my father, someone renowned for his honesty and integrity, who asserts that he had never met Wally Clayton, this man to whom he was supposed to have been passing secrets.

In the 1990s when you were researching *Breaking the Codes*, did you think to interview my dad and hear his side of the story?

Did you bother reading the evidence in his book *My Father's Son – the last knot untied* where Alan Renouf, former Secretary of the Department of Foreign Affairs, stated that 'the reason [for his failure to get a security clearance] had nothing whatsoever to do with Throssell's loyalty, judgement or competence.'

And yes, I did know you at the ANU when you were in your left-wing phase, and am quite intrigued by the fact that you 'cannot believe that I could have served Wally Clayton's agenda.' Why ever not? After all, I not only had parents who you were happy to accept were spies, despite all other evidence to the contrary; happy to keep the press forever searching for reds under the bed, and ruin their lives in the process. Why not keep it going with the third generation?

It makes just as much sense.

Yours sincerely, Karen Throssell

ITEM #93

Wally Clayton

Wally Clayton, Wally Clayton,
doesn't sound like a spy.
No glamour, no drama,
no Burgess or Blunt.

More friendly than 'Walter',
a name for a wombat,
or a frivolous fool who
gets lost or wastes water.

But with you, it was true –
not a Clayton a Clayton
you were fair dinkum
and proud of it too.

Did you need Clayton's comrades?
Was there none that was real?
Was it lonely up there
on the ideologue's perch?

Was a 'nest' of you better
with Wally, head viper?[1]
Surely more scary
than a solitary snake?

Or did someone put
those names in your mouth?
A Clayton's researcher,
you thought you could trust?

---

1 *Nest of traitors* refers to the book about Clayton's spy ring by Whitlam and Stubbs.

A Cold War Warrior –
with his chain and his Ball?
Spy-ring-a-rosie,
watch them all fall.

Or did you really believe
that they were all yours?
Paranoid delusions –
the old spy psychosis.

Dobbed them in,
on your deathbed.
A-tissue a-tissue
they all fall down.

ITEM #94

Soviet spies had protection in very high places

THE WEEKEND AUSTRALIAN, JANUARY 14-15, 2012
www.theaustralian.com.au

Soviet spies had protection in very high places

Beneath Canberra's sleepy surface in the 1940s were concealed some explosive secrets

DESMOND BALL

CORAL Bell is one of the world's foremost academic experts on international relations, crisis management. House, in Canberra. "In those days we were a very small group," she says.

Professor). At one of the lunches with Throssell, Hill and Rose in late 1947, after they had finished eating, Throssell said to Bell: "Some of us think that the Soviet Union ought to see these documents". Bell says: "I assumed he was joking, so I laughed merrily, and said something to the effect that it sounded like a splendid way

Desmond Ball in *The Australian*:

> Coral Bell, one of the world's foremost academic experts on international relations...began her career in international politics in the Australian Diplomatic Service, joining the Department of External Affairs as a diplomatic cadet in Canberra in 1945.
>
> Over the next three years, she got to know well several members of the department who were spying for the Soviet Union, especially Jim Hill (code-named Tourist) and Ric Throssell (Ferro).
>
> She is absolutely persuaded that John Burton, the head of the department 'provided top cover' for the spies. She believes that an attempt was made to recruit her in late 1947, and that her caustic response caused Burton to move quickly to sideline her in the department...
>
> In 1946, Bell was assigned to the department's UN division, of which Burton was then the head, as well as being head of the entire department. Here she formed a close relationship with Hill and Throssell, her senior colleagues in the division.
>
> 'I used to bring sandwiches for lunch, and eat them on the West Block lawn. And much of the time I had very pleasant company in the shape of three agreeable young men, Jim Hill, Ric Throssell, and Fred Rose....'

[Rose] also worked for Soviet intelligence (code-named Professor). At one of the lunches...in late 1947, after they had finished eating, Throssell said to Bell, 'Some of us think that the Soviet Union ought to see these documents'. Bell says: 'I assumed he was joking, so I laughed merrily and said something to the effect that it sounded like a splendid way to get oneself into jail.'

Bell believes that Throssell told Burton of her 'frivolous' response and that Burton 'acted fast' to remove her from his central policy division... 'only a few months after that I was 'posted' to the Australian office in New Zealand...'

[Bell later commented]: 'I might have been initially seen as a possible recruit to the cause by Ric and Fred and Jim (and others higher up)' and that she 'had disappointed that expectation with my light-hearted remark about jail.'...

Bell believes that Burton was more involved with Soviet intelligence than merely his 'top-cover' role.

In particular, she has considered the possibility that Burton was the principal contact of the head of the Soviet Military Intelligence (GRU) office in the Canberra embassy, Victor Zaitsev. She says 'I wouldn't be in the least surprised.'

Bell recalls [Fred] Rose with some fondness. She says he was 'such a nice person' and 'very charming'. She went to parties at his house in Turner, which were also attended by Throssell and Hill. In 1948–50, this house was the main 'drop' used by the spies in External Affairs to leave documents and other material for collection by Clayton. For the previous three years, Clayton had used a flat in Braddon, occupied by Throssell in 1947–49, for this purpose.

Bell believes that 'The truly tragic figure in all this was to my mind Ric Throssell. When I first knew him, around 1947, he was a handsome young man with apparently everything to live for, and prospects of rising to whatever eminence he wanted, either in diplomacy or politics, or even literature. He used to read to us, during those lunchtimes, bits of a play he was writing, all about atomic weapons and such.'

ITEM #95

Dr John Burton

John Burton in the 1980s

In his *Australian* 14 January 2012 article, Ball focused on a new target. No longer satisfied with junior diplomats, he was after the scalp of the Head of the External Affairs Department – John Burton. But he didn't stop there. Ball was later to cast aspersions on no less than the Leader of the Labor Opposition – Dr Herbert Vere Evatt.

According to Phillip Adams, John Burton was 'probably the most visionary and controversial public servant of the twentieth century.'

To law academic Dr Gregory Tillet, he was a 'towering intellect whose extraordinary genius laid the intellectual and scholarly foundation for the study of conflict resolution.'

To Norman Abjorensen, he was 'one of our great unsung heroes, who brought intellectual rigour to bear on foreign policy.'

For the colonialist conservatives in the foreign affairs business, he was ahead of his time. Hs main crime was to question 'Australia's links with Britain and the United States, advocating instead a foreign policy based on Australia developing a better understanding of and engagement with our Asian neighbours.' He wanted to support Indonesian independence from Holland; challenged the belief that China was inextricably tied to the Soviet Union and thus forever our enemy; and was instrumental in setting up the Colombo Plan, which aimed to promote international efforts to raise the living standards of people in South and South East Asia.

There were two similarities between Ball's attacks on Burton and those on my father. They were both based on completely unsubstantiated claims; and Ball waited until his targets were dead before launching his attack.

This time, Ball's target was not only a highly respected public figure; his daughter was no mere small-time poet to whom the media could repeatedly refuse the right of reply, but a highly qualified lawyer and academic they couldn't ignore.

Burton's daughter, Pamela Burton, launched her highly detailed and scholarly rebuttal of Ball's assertions in a 2014 essay for *Honest History*.

ITEM #96

Pamela Burton

It is an unenviable task defending a parent against an opponent as well placed as Des Ball AO. He has been labelled as 'the man who saved the world from nuclear annihilation' by former US President Jimmy Carter and acclaimed for the brave work he has done in Cambodia.

ITEM # 97

What can children do to destroy the credibility of those who have maligned their parents?

Pamela Burton makes many points that are of equal relevance to both our fathers' histories at the hands of Des Ball.

The way John Burton has been treated by the political right is a case study of how a distorted picture of someone can be built up over time by commentators willing to undermine someone because of what they stand for.

My father was more a victim of guilt by association – the man who had a mother – and by circumstance: the man with the communist mother, who was posted to Russia. Burton, on the other hand, was targeted for his beliefs – his radical approach to foreign policy in an era of paranoid conservatism, along with a bit of guilt by association – his supposed protection of the 'real reds' in his department.

The conservatives had a mantra: *If you are not with us, you are against us, and if you are against us you are our enemy*. In those days, communists were the new enemy, and suspicion fell on all radical thinkers.

As well as putting Des Ball's behaviour into some context, Pamela Burton also exposes the methodology of defamation:

> Putting made-up words in someone's mouth and then leaving it up to the targets to 'prove' they never said them, is…one of the many 'weapons of mass destruction' that word-tricksters deploy.

Ball quotes Bell, who claims to be quoting Ric Throssell as saying: 'Some of us think the Soviet Union ought to see these documents.' Even if he hadn't been 12 years dead, my father could still not 'prove' that he didn't say them, other than calling on now dead witnesses. Possibly, the unlikelihood of 'these' (indicating that they were present) highly classified documents being out on the lawns with them at lunchtime could raise a question about the veracity of the statement? However, to use the 'unlikelihood of' and 'raising a question' has us using the same lack of rigour as Ms Bell.

Given my own desire to confront Ball and demand answers, I was delighted to read that Pamela Burton had actually succeeded in bailing him up in the kitchen at a Canberra party:

> Terrible behaviour on my part, but I was angry and I wanted an apology and a 'please explain' from him.

In particular, she quizzed him on his misquotation of John Burton in the Royal Commission, something she was able to point out with a direct reference to the transcript itself. When she pointed out that he had clearly got it wrong, Ball denied it and then avoided any scrutiny by announcing that 'his sources were too secret' to be revealed.

So what he implied was that he never used the public record. He only relied on secret material; material not available to anyone else.

This could explain why he ignored the findings of the Royal Commission about my father. He had never read them. And we will never find out what his 'secret sources' were, if they ever really existed.

Pamela Burton had more success quizzing Ball about Coral Bell's 'evidence'. Ball had apparently mentioned Bell's self-confessed lust for (the handsome and charming) Ric Throssell and Jim Hill. Pamela put it to Ball that Coral Bell could also have lusted after the charming and handsome Head of Department, John Burton, who not only rejected her advances, but sent her packing to New Zealand. Ball agreed. He said, 'She said as much.'

At least Coral Bell had a reason (though no justification) for telling lies. Ball not only used the spurious evidence of a woman scorned; he could possibly have even suggested the idea to her. Pamela Burton points out that Bell was not in Australia, nor in the Department of External Affairs, when allegations of leaking documents surfaced.

ITEM #98

I, too, attempted yet again to put my father's case in a reply to the article in *The Australian*. Once again, they refused to publish.

Old lies, new targets

(unpublished)

Dear Sir,

In 1996 this paper was forced, by the threat of a libel suit, to apologise to the Throssell family, for using a front-page photo of my parents alongside the words Soviet Spies. In the apology, on page 14, the paper stated that the Venona decrypts had established that Throssell had not been a member of a spy ring.

Now, 12 years after my parents' death, Des Ball doesn't even use the word allege... Regardless of the Venona decrypts and the apology, he asserts they were all spying for the Soviet Union.

This article is primarily about his new target, Dr John Burton. My father and his colleagues are merely referred to as *the spies*. Although there was a new allegation: that Ric's home in Braddon was occupied for the purpose of a 'document drop' for Clayton's spy ring.

I was born in 1948. This little flat in Braddon was my first home. Somehow newborn babies and spy dens seem an unlikely combination.

When the Royal Commission into Espionage was set up, Burton was not a suspect, but he gave evidence in camera. He was not convinced that those targeted by the inquiry were Soviet agents, particularly Ric Throssell and Jim Hill.

As Pamela Burton argues in her lecture for *Honest History*, John Burton's defence of them was the basis of Ball's suspicions about him.

In this article, Ball's only 'evidence' is the 1947 recollections of Coral Bell, her conversations over sandwiches on the lawns outside West Block, and her belief that my father was responsible for her removal from the Department of External Affairs (for her refusal to become a spy). Des Ball describes her as 'one of the world's foremost academic experts on international relations.' For such an esteemed academic, her comments are curiously vague and anecdotal, with a complete lack of supporting evidence.

1

Submitted to *The Australian* 15 January 2012

She 'believes'…even 'firmly believes'; is 'absolutely persuaded'; she 'considered the possibility'; 'wouldn't be the least surprised'… She also, again given her serious academic reputation, has a strange fixation with the fact that all her young male colleagues – Throssell, Hill, and Fred Rose – were 'handsome and charming,' a phrase she uses several times.

And then we have the strangely truncated conclusion to the article where Bell laments the 'truly tragic figure' of the (handsome, charming) Throssell with apparently everything to live for.

Bell doesn't explain why his life became 'truly tragic'. But I can.

Ric Throssell did have 'so much to live for'…until his life was dogged and his career stymied by the machinations of ASIO and the persistent defamatory accusations of unscrupulous muckrakers like Des Ball.

Yours sincerely,

Karen Throssell, Warrandyte

ITEM #99

truth

(n.) 1. in accordance with fact or reality.
2. a true theory is congruent with our experience.

# ITEM #100

The death of Des Ball

Des Ball died the week this manuscript was shortlisted for a literary prize... the week it became more likely that finally the truth could be told.

Part of me was relieved that he was now unable to sue me, or at least start a new barrage of *Throssell, Spy* articles in *The Australian, The Sun* or *The Courier Mail*.

But part of me had always wanted to talk to him – confront him, go to his house and say:

> *Why the fuck? You are contradicting the findings of a Royal Commission; the Venona decrypts; contradicting many highly esteemed lawyers, historians, politicians, judges and diplomats – even the few journalists who are not bound to their ideological masters...and of course the lifelong outpourings of your victims.*
>
> *But as a rusted-on Cold War warrior still looking for reds under the bed when the rest of the paranoid right are looking for Muslims under the mattress, you have risked making yourself a laughing stock among even much of the conservative academic establishment. You are seriously compromising your own distinguished academic reputation by failing to be diligent and accurate with your research, by constantly repeating unsubstantiated claims, and your cowardly avoidance of your victims, refusing to allow them to ever have any right of reply.*

From his obituaries, it appeared that it was not dad who wore the Janus mask, as Ball claimed, but Mr Ball himself. I began to question my description of him as a 'dishonest unprincipled man.' So many of the obituaries (albeit from the conservative academic and defence establishment) were so contrary to my knowledge of him through his actions and his writing. His research and teaching were characterised by 'exhaustive field-based study motivated by a deep passion and concern for human well-being and justice.' Justice! I knew that he was highly regarded in defence and strategic studies circles, but the frequent references to his 'meticulous research' were even less surprising than the discussion of his politics. He went from being a 'person of interest' to ASIO, to become a harsh critic of their incompetence. His critical stance on our subservient position in the Australia–US Alliance and his avowed opposition to nuclear war made him a different Des Ball from the one who had perpetrated such prolonged injustice against my father and others.

A couple of years earlier, I had seen a program on the ABC about Ball's work on the Thai–Myanmar border in defence of the Karens' fight for independence. Had he become some sort of bleeding heart pinko? Starting to think about real people? That's when I thought I should visit. Maybe he had developed a social conscience? Or any kind of conscience…

We were once comrades: fellow anti-Vietnam War activists in the sixties. Our group at the ANU was tiny. I can still almost name them all. Megan Stoyles is a lifelong labour activist and was the *Make love not War* t-shirt woman whose photo appeared in *Life* magazine; Helen Jarvis is a highly regarded academic expert on South-East Asian politics; John Iremonger was one of the founders of Hale and Iremonger Press; and Des Ball. At that first demo in Garema Place, where some jeering shoppers encircled and attacked us, ignored by the cops – we should have been bonded by the experience?

And some of us undoubtedly were.

I have an academic research background and a mother who was a philosopher. She taught us always to question. So, of course, Ball created a question – for a fleeting moment.

It is so hard to understand what possible reason there could be, even for an ex or continuing CIA agent, for the man whom they described after his death as an upright and caring citizen, to be obsessed by old history and a dead suspect, in a climate where there are very different bogey men. So you do find yourself questioning certainties.

What if Des Ball did know something we didn't know, and our dad's acting skill enabled him to create a totally false persona? Could this wonderful man, full of wisdom, compassion and integrity, have been a sham? Just an actor, who fooled even his family?

But our very canny mother certainly wasn't someone who could have been fooled. Maybe she was in on it too? Are you insinuating two sham parents, Des Ball?

No, his poison hasn't even touched the surface. We were a very close family, and we knew each other extremely well. Especially dad, who was a guts-spiller. Not only did he write two autobiographies and a biography of his mother; he was always telling us stories about his life, his ideas, his highs and lows. There are also numerous albums full of his beautiful black-and-white photos, documenting this life from his earliest years – including that tragic, falsely incriminating year in Russia.

He wore his heart on his sleeve. Couldn't contain tears, anger, hilarity, scorn. A terrible poker player. He was a crier. He would cry laughing, especially when he'd had a drink; his face would redden, the tears would flow – it was the blubbering Irish in him. Dad, a spy? Impossible.

So our certainties stay certainties. We know, deep in our bones, that our father was just as he seemed. No sham. No secret fucking spy. And not just our beloved father, but an extraordinary human being, like his mum. Someone with the qualities and courage most mere mortals – including Professor Ball, 'public intellectual' – could never approach.

ITEM #101

... I wish I wish he'd go away

> Yesterday upon the stair,
> I met a man who wasn't there
> He wasn't there again today
> I wish, I wish he'd go away...
>
> WILLIAM HUGHES MEARNS

I finally realise they weren't interested in truth

The ethics of these men remains to be addressed

They just want names – likely names

These diligent men do not want to know

The ethics of these men remains to be addressed

Always beyond, the unspoken story, the unconfirmed report

These diligent men do not want to know

And you can't defame the dead

Somewhere beyond, the unspoken story the undisclosed report
Surely no one believes I am a Russian spy
Of course you can't defame the dead
The world turns on the whispers of the Fourth Estate

Surely no one believes I am some sort of spy
Those hidden men, those judging men
The world turns on the whispers of the Fourth Estate
Both press statements are the opposite of the truth

Those hidden men, those judging men
I begin to see myself as the man they created
They report the opposite of what was said
Turn and they are gone

I begin to see myself as the man they created
Again I appeal, again I lose
Turn and they are gone
It's bloody disgraceful what they've done to you

Again I appeal, again I lose
They just want names – likely names
It's bloody disgraceful what they've done to you
I finally realise they aren't interested in truth

ITEM #102

Not bravery

(2001)

He was so brave they said.
Brave – not a word I'd use.
Death was a beacon:

the promise of a warm fire
at the end of a long road;
the prospect of release

from present pain;
from the gnawing fear
of future decline;

and the thought of life
without life's companion.
Not bravery.

Maybe bravery to those who saw
defiance of the law as brave.
But you spent your life

defying unjust laws.
Now guided by love, fear, escape
not bravery

Brave would be to stay for us –
your children and our own.
We thought we'd always be

cloaked in the comfort
of your wisdom
your love.

The world's a lesser place
without him, said those
who also called you brave.

This imperfect world
you pit yourself to change
still needs that rare integrity.

So ignore the pleas
of selfish children.
Think not of us

and our diminished world.
Think of your fight for peace
and the future of all children...

But maybe,
to give this up, and us,
knowing how you cared;

the fighter giving up the fight
that was your life.
Maybe they were right –

It was bravery.

Dad left us too early. And the poem above shows that, for a while, I was hurt and angry that he chose to die with my mother when she was diagnosed with an inoperable brain tumour. So we were to lose them both.

Dad, how could you leave us too?

We knew they made a pact to 'go together'. Such was the strength of their bond, that dad couldn't bear the thought of living without his beloved Dodie.

But I also think that he might have been really sick of the struggle. Imagine enduring 50 years of media pillorying and career stagnation *after* undergoing the trauma of a Royal Commission which completely exonerated you. Imagine all those years of knowing no one was listening, no one cared.

No one except a few Cold War warriors whose entire raison d'être was the continual search for reds under the bed.

I look at the two photos of dad again, the last one taken the year before he died, still with the cloud over his name. He was 76, these days too young to die, and I believe he had at least a good 15 years left. And they would have been good years, if the truth had been told and, finally, *the man who wasn't there* was the one who met an appropriate end.

ITEM #103

Certainties

        Freeways, though often controversial
        at their inception are usually the fastest way
        to move large volumes of traffic over long stretches

The trip takes two hours door to door
give or take time for works
on the Western Ring Road

You take a hundred km per hour for granted
and time your dinner at the other end
on that assumption

        I'm sitting on the freeway, writing...
        we are crawling at about 1 km per hour
        it's Friday – three lanes, grumpily sardined

They say 'nothing's certain except death'
Taxes are the only certainty and then
if you're not rich or very poor.

I don't believe it – we need it
Certainly equals stability.
We need a few things to hold on to
to stay grounded, sane?

If there were no certainties wouldn't we fracture,
fragment – little pieces of us fly away?

        Huge smash – peak hour, five cars, someone trapped.
        Someone dead. And I'm worrying about
        being late for dinner, and the end of that little certainty

God is certainty
'Watching over us' –
a how, and why?

Does that mean sceptics
don't need certainties?
or do they find others?

And what if certainties
are at odds?
Like god always on 'our' side?

        The traffic's moving
        we're being re-routed off the freeway
        by frazzled but patient police

Sun, sea, seasons – certainties?
The sun will rise, set
sometimes wondrously announcing arrivals, departures –

or hiding behind grey veils
or relentless – parching, searing, cracking
Some, in deserts may wish for less certainty

Whilst man has spoked the season's wheel
longer, hotter, wetter, wilder...seasons are still there,
with the sea, always washing in its wide blue wisdom

        Cars sidle into narrower lanes,
        clogging up suburban streets
        weary fingers drumming on roof tops

Eat, sleep, procreate, die
All problematic, can all be done well or not
but they are in fact inevitable – certain

Of course there will always be
love or lust – sex and babies
And don't all mothers love them

even if it is only hormonal – an instinct for survival?
And don't children love or grow to love, their mothers
and fathers, mostly...

> ringing home (or busily writing)
> small dramas within small spaces, all wishing
> for the certainty of somewhere-else?

But maybe we can only be specific
So many unloved babies,
embattled families

My family was full of love – full of certainties.
You could feel it in Dad's huge hugs
Mum's patient listening, her quiet generosity.

We were such challenging kids
shop-lifting, drug-taking, school-wagging
Still, they were always there

> They're polite, these drivers, leaving gaps for new cars
> to squeeze into the creeping queue
> the certainty of kindness?

All our family rituals: Dad setting the table
 the night before breakfast
before the cup of tea in bed with
squares of brown bread and butter

You breathed in that love, knew it was
all-encompassing, all forgiving
always there –

> and then we're free—
> the alternative route wide and empty
> one hundred kms per hour and home – to a kind of certainty

BIOGRAPHY OF RIC THROSSELL

In a way, this whole book is a biography of my father. While the focus was on the part of his life as a scapegoat – an innocent pawn in a much bigger political game – I did endeavour to reveal the whole man as well, the man whose beliefs and values would not have allowed him to be a spy.

Ric was born in in 1922 in Greenmount WA (on the kitchen table, so the family mythology goes). His parents were renowned writer and founding member of the Communist Party of Australia, Katharine Susannah Prichard, and equally renowned Gallipoli hero and VC winner Hugo Vivian Hope (Jim) Throssell. Hugo was the youngest of 11 children; his father, George Throssell, started off as a small-time grocer in the goldfields town of Northam and ended up so successful a businessman that he was said to run the town. George earned himself the name of 'The Lion of Avon' after the river that runs through the town.

Hugo and Katharine were married in 1918. They were an unconventional couple: Katharine was a feisty, left-wing novelist, and Hugo was the well-off son of a conservative businessman. Because Hugo was expected to be involved in the Throssell grocery empire, he had little employment training; after he married, he made his way with a variety of jobs, the main one being real estate. Katharine was most often the breadwinner, although a writer's income was even more meagre and unpredictable then than it is today. Hugo was a dreamer and renowned for trying a range of get-rich-quick schemes. As the

Depression hit, this became harder and harder. When Katharine was overseas on a writing trip in 1933, Hugo became very financially desperate and tried to pawn his VC. He was offered 10 shillings for it but declined. Later that year, Hugo committed suicide. In his farewell note, he hoped that his wife and young son would be better off with a war widow's pension.

Ric was the only child. He experienced an idyllic childhood in the bush of Greenmount. After his beloved father's suicide, he and Katharine battled on together until he left for boarding school.

Ric was educated at Wesley College (Perth), thanks to the generosity of one of his father's soldier mates. He planned to become a teacher, but this was cut short by war. Ric served as a linesman in Papua New Guinea and from there applied to be a diplomatic cadet, arriving in Canberra in 1943 when he was 22.

Like his mother, Ric had a huge commitment to social justice in general and to the peace movement in particular. He believed that we are on this earth to make a difference. His life reflected her belief that the personal is political and that every action must be congruent with your values. And, like Katharine, I'm sure that he would want to be remembered for his 'being' – his ideas and values – as well as his 'doing' – his more tangible achievements.

The theatre was a lifelong passion for Ric. Speakers at his funeral paid tribute to his meticulous, exacting and ruthless directing and his towering, magnificent performances. In a letter to *The Canberra Times*, Manning Clark said that dad's interpretation of King Lear 'will live for a long time in the minds of those who, like me, had the good fortune to see it.'

Over the years, Ric wrote 26 plays, many of which reflected his concern with peace. *For Valour* was based on the life of his father. The theme of *Valley of the Shadows* was the hysterical blindness of an Australian soldier as a symbol of the world closing its eyes to the drift towards war. *Legend* was a Cold War love story with an anti-war message. Particularly important was *The Day before Tomorrow.* An anti-nuclear play way before its time, it was chosen to be performed at the Olympic Village in Melbourne in 1956.

Don Batchelor has written comprehensively on the contribution of Ric Throssell to Australian theatre, as a playwright, a director and an actor.

Ric later moved to writing non-fiction, including his biography of Katharine, *Wild Weeds and Windflowers*. Probably his best-known work is his autobiography, *My Father's Son,* which was shortlisted for the Banjo Award.

Ric also wrote four novels which, to some extent, represent a return to the social realism that was evident in most of his plays. His last major work, *Tomorrow,* explores the Communist Party's appeal to some when, for many, the division between ideals and reality had grown to become a chasm. Many thought that the book reflected Ric's disillusion with the models so fiercely defended by Katharine.

While Ric was not a pacifist (he always said he'd kill in defence of his loved ones, and he did serve as a soldier in New Guinea in the Second World War), he was a staunch activist and campaigner for the peace movement.

His fellow peace activists in People for Nuclear Disarmament and Writers against Nuclear Arms spoke at his funeral about his ready availability to give talks at a range of different venues, from schools to the Australian Defence Force Academy, and his considerable diplomatic skills, which were helpful in fundraising and organising. They were particularly impressed with his willingness to do behind the scenes work, such as trooping tirelessly to bookshops and libraries.

There was also the dramatic television sale of his father's VC in 1985 to raise money for the peace movement. Recalling Hugo's profound disillusionment with war after his return from Gallipoli, dad had asked us kids whether we minded losing our 'inheritance'. He said that Hugo would have approved of using his medal to promote the message of peace.

Ironically. it was the Returned and Services League (RSL) that bought the medal. Dad used the money to make a film called *The Pursuit of Happiness*, a powerful short film directed by Martha Ansara. The film had only limited distribution, mostly to people already committed to the cause. However, dad made sure that the book I wrote to accompany the film was placed in schools and libraries. He visited all the high schools in Canberra personally to convince them that they needed it, spreading the peace message as far as he could.

Dad spent most of his working life as a Canberra public servant, and the present book largely deals with the negatives of this life – the constant frustrations and obstacles created by his failure to obtain an ASIO security clearance, which prevented him from having the career path he wished for.

Nonetheless, there were considerable achievements.

Greg O'Reardon, a colleague when dad was the Head of the International Training Branch of the Department of External Affairs, praised his distinguished contribution to Australia's foreign aid program, stressing the fact that he converted a minor extension of Australian foreign policy into Australia's most extensive, concrete and beneficial international relations program ever.

Dad once talked to me about his early role with Evatt and the United Nations. This may have been the beginning of his peace activism, though his views were formed long before, knowing his father's passionate anti-war stance as a returned soldier. In *My Father's Son*, he writes about relishing his work, convinced that the United Nations could bring peace and security to the world. Ric was a strong supporter of the role of the UN as a peacekeeper. He played an important role in the ending of the Dutch police action in Indonesia, with the adoption of the Australian resolution to the Security Council of the UN to end the fighting between the Dutch and the Indonesians. He says in *My Father's Son*: 'I felt as though I had made some contribution to peace in our part of the world.'

In the present book, I have tried to show the private side of the public man, from my own perspective. The fact that I spent 10 years of my life trying to do what he had not been able to do – clear his name – is testimony to the wonderful father he was. He was also grandfather to my two daughters, Katie and Bry, and to my sister Keedah's two boys, Remy and Floyd. He was adored by them all.

Katie wrote this very soon after Ric's death in 1999:

> In his workroom the smell of leather and varnish, each tool hung
>
> carefully on its own peg. *A place for everything and everything in its place.* He had sayings for every occasion, ever ready with a lesson on the important things in life. Even as a small child I was not spared these lectures. He believed that discussion of the morality of one's actions at age four would make a difference – perhaps it did. I used to hate these talks, and the way he made me always look at him in the eyes. He had very brown eyes. Today I'd give anything to hold his hand and talk of things, done and seen without him.
>
> The best thing in this room is the table, still piled high with papers, scraps filled with roughly scrawled ideas. Surveying his table, his workspace, I see a man who was both productive and creative, who wrote about politics as often as he wrote plays. Everything here is just as he left it. I fancy that if I don't disturb anything, I may hear his footfall up the path, and see him in the doorway, with his brown eyes and his crooked smile.
>
> There must be a million books on these shelves, on everything from politics to poetry, science to Shakespeare. This is how I remember him, as the learned man. The man to come to for help with literature, drama, or creative writing. The man for inspiration and interpretation.

He baked me rock cakes the day he died. There are two left – no-one wanted to eat them so they are very hard. I hold one in my hand, as he did yesterday. I eat it and cry, salt mingled with sugar. My teeth hurt but I keep eating until there is nothing left, then I cry more.

My grandfather, the writer, the actor, the man who loved making jam and rock cakes. King of this house, once king of my world. Now gone.

No tribute to dad would be complete without mentioning our beloved mother Dodie – his 'other half'. Normally, I would never use this term, but in their case it was apt. Dad was a totally devoted husband and a true romantic. Mum was his adviser, his muse, his calm centre, his loyal comrade and the love of his life – and he knew he couldn't live without her.

Strong believers in one's right to control the time and manner of one's own death, they chose to go together after Mum was diagnosed with a terminal brain tumour. Ric and Dodie died on 30 April 1999.

THE WRITING JOURNEY

In about 2009 when I showed my now good friend and mentor, John Jenkins, some of my poems about my father's experience as an innocent man accused of being a spy, he said You should do something with all this stuff – people need to know… But I didn't act on it until 2011 when a friend alerted me to a newspaper article by Gerard Henderson which repeated the untrue misinformation that had dogged my parents during their lifetime.

After several more newspaper articles, newspaper refusals to publish my letters, and many angry poems, I started re-reading dad's history of the period. I also started to research the history of the 1955 Royal Commission on Espionage and the ways in which it affected my father's life.

John initially suggested writing a play, but this was my father's field, not mine. But I thought maybe there were some scriptwriting genes there somewhere, and I enlisted the help of WA playwright and friend Suzanne Inglebrecht. We spent a month in the summer of 2013 turning my material into a script, which we submitted to the Australia Council for the Arts for a grant. It was a good submission, but it was an Abbott government. When it was rejected, we consoled ourselves with the idea that it was too politically 'hot'. We should wait for a more conducive political climate to submit again. This was to be a sadly echoing refrain through the 10-year journey of this manuscript.

So I went back to my comfort zone and concentrated on my now evolving format of collage – poetry and prose, letters, articles and quotes.

I soon discovered that this style wasn't my quirky invention – it had a name: Creative Non-Fiction. *Good: I had a box to put most of my non-straight poetry writing in.*

With another piece of writing in the same vein (a book about feminist and trade union responses to part-time work), I attended a six-month series of workshops run by the inimitable Jeff Sparrow and gained a lot of ideas for this current book too.

In 2015, I started the editing process, focusing on the poetry with the help of one of my poetry heroes, Jordie Albiston. We had been incredibly fortunate at the Neighbourhood House where I worked to have Jordie as a poetry tutor. As a result, we were the first, and I suspect the only, Neighbourhood House in the state of Victoria – if not the whole of Australia – to have three full poetry classes running while she was there.

Jordie has an extraordinary list of poetry awards and nominations over the years, culminating in winning the Patrick White Award for her contribution to Australian literature in 2019. And she was a very generous and exacting editor. Over several months, I made the train journey across Melbourne from Warrandyte to Jordie's house in Altona. She helped edit the poetry and was instrumental in my understanding of the importance of layout and the marrying of form to content. It was exemplified by her early book, *The Hanging of Jean Lee* – telling the history of Victoria's first woman to be hanged – which was not only written in poetry, but set out like the sensational newspapers that salaciously followed her life. So the story of her birth and death were written as newspaper birth and death notices, and the story of her tragic life had sensational newspaper headings throughout.

In the same vein, I decided to make my work look like an official bureaucratic document or scrap book, with numbered 'items' and a lot of white space to distinguish different 'documents'.

In 2015, I saw an ad for a workshop on *How to pitch your MS* with a group of WA publishers at Katharine Susannah Prichard House (the home of my late grandmother in the hills outside of Perth, which has now become a writers' centre). Always keen for an excuse to visit one of my 'heart places', I decided to get the MS ready to pitch. But what was a 'pitch'? I'd never had to do that before with the poetry books I had published…

Like many writers, I regularly met with other writer friends to discuss and workshop current projects. These friends, especially John Jenkins and Carmel Macdonald Grahame, were invaluable in the process of editing and re-editing this story.

In one of these sessions, Anne Connor, a friend with a background in PR, offered to show me the basics of pitching to prepare me for this endeavour.

And it worked! For UWAP at least. Terri-Anne White (former publisher and director of University of Western Australia Press) was very enthusiastic and encouraged me to send them the full MS. I did, and I also submitted it to their new award for an unpublished work of creative non-fiction, the Dorothy

Hewett Award. To my amazement, in 2016 it was shortlisted! After the Award ceremony, Terri-Anne took me aside and said that it largely didn't win because there wasn't enough of it; it needed to be longer.

So, back to the drawing board. I decided to include more historical information. In 2017, I enlisted the help of Professor of Australian History Philip Deery, who was an invaluable source of information and advice about the existing content. We met monthly for the next couple of years until I resubmitted the now much longer MS to UWAP. I also enlisted another friend and professional copy editor, Nan McNab, who worked on it after all the new material had been included. I submitted it again in September 2018. When I hadn't heard anything by March the next year, I rang to enquire as to its fate. The reply was strange: they told me that they didn't know how to market it, so they couldn't publish it.

Of course, I was very disappointed. But after licking my wounds for a few months, I rallied and started sending the manuscript out to potential publishers. From one after another, I got similar responses: after lavish praise about the writing and the timeliness of the material, they declined – mostly with excuses about difficulty in marketing.

So, again, the manuscript was assigned to the 'almost given up drawer'. Then, in late 2019, a friend suggested a small alternative publisher who might be interested. The rest is history. When I approached Janey Stone from Interventions with my history of rejection, remarking that they were probably scared of the politics, her wonderful answer was that Interventions exists to publish books like this.

．．．．．．．

This book grew over a long period, and there is a host of people to thank. The same people who got me started also kept me going through the highs and lows of the 10-year writing journey – especially my wonderful friend Carmel Macdonald Grahame. John Jenkins was there from the beginning and was closely involved in our group workshopping sessions. The creative friendship of these two, their inspiration, encouragement and staying power, made all the difference. Other friends in writing groups I have been part of were also important, and I give huge thanks to Cheryl Simpson, Anne Connor and Cathy Hainstock.

There were other people along the way, like Susanne Inglebrecht, who gave early support for the project. Jeff Sparrow, whose writing has inspired me for a long time, was also a highly skilled teacher of creative non-fiction. He sowed early seeds about the genre that I have learned to love. Jeff also told me that I should 'write about my family!'

Jordie Albiston, my poetry editor, was important in the editing of the poetry and was critical in the development of the format and layout of the book. I feel privileged to have a poet of such calibre involved in this project. Phillip Deery shared his formidable knowledge of the history and people who played an important role in Australia's own McCarthy era over many wonderful Greek meals with a few bottles of red. Nan McNab was scrupulous in her copy editing, and her gentle but significant suggestions over several years and several versions have made a real difference.

This list of thankyous is a testimony to the value of friendship; even my professional helpers forgave me after the exhausting process of editing and became good friends.

I'm grateful too to Terri-Anne White, from the University of WA Press, who gave the early manuscript a warm reception. Being shortlisted for the Dorothy Hewett prize really boosted my confidence. If I hadn't taken her advice to double the size of the MS, it probably wouldn't have reached this final complete version.

Mei Yen Chua of Swallow Books helped with structural editing over the autumn of 2020, supported by a grant from the Perth branch of the Australian Society for the Study of Labour History. Melbourne's extended lockdown during 2020 was both a boon (all that time to edit!) and a frustration (having to communicate remotely, slowing down the process). Mei Yen and I wrote from our remote homes in genuine isolation (me in the bush in the Yarra Valley outside Melbourne, and she in southern Tasmania). We got to know one another by sharing tips on growing vegetables and recipes for the more exotic ones, as well as gloomy weather discussions, oh, and editing work too. I felt sad that I couldn't go and visit, see her wonderful garden, and discuss the manuscript properly!

But of course it is Janey Stone, Eris Harrison, Lisa Milner and the rest of the team from Interventions whom I have to thank, for having confidence in the project. They not only recognised the importance of getting my father's story out there; they appreciated the unorthodox form and were not intimidated by poetry!

And a special thanks to the fabulous graphic designer Viktoria Ivanova for understanding so well the importance of marrying the layout to the content, for her skill in using the many graphics she was showered with, and for loving lots of white space!

I am thankful that courageous and truly independent publishers like Interventions still exist and in fact flourish in these straitened times, and I encourage you all to support their wonderful work.

SOURCES

QUOTES

All quotes from Ric Throssell are taken from his own writings, either from *My Father's Son* (revised edition) or from unpublished material in the possession of Karen Throssell. His quoted words are set out in white inside black boxes, suggesting the notion of redacted text in an ASIO document.

Quotes from Dodie Throssell are taken from her diaries.

Words attributed to Katharine Susannah Pritchard in #12 Postcards from Russia are loosely adapted from her book, *The Real Russia*, Modern Publishers, 1935.

All use of bold format within quotes is by the author, unless otherwise indicated.

All definitions are from Macquarie Dictionary online.

OTHER WORKS

Abjorensen, Norman, 'A victim of intelligence game', *Canberra Times*, 8 October 1996.

Ackland, Richard, 'Judging Dyson Heydon', *The Saturday Paper*, 22 August 2015.

Ball, Desmond & Horner, David Murray, *Breaking the Codes: Australia's KGB Network 1944–1950*, Allen & Unwin, 1998.

Brown, Wilton John (ed.), *The Petrov Conspiracy Unmasked: ASIO's Criminal Activities Revealed; Watergate in Australia*, also titled *The Petrov Commission Unmasked*, Melbourne, Communist Party of Australia (Marxist-Leninist), 1973.

Burton, Pamela, 'John Burton: Undermined by Dishonest History', *Honest History*, 1 September 2014.

Carter, Miranda, *Anthony Blunt – His Lives*, Farrar, Strauss and Giroux, 2001.

Crozier, Lorna, 'Facts about my father', in *The Blue Hour of the Day: Selected Poems*, McClelland & Stewart, 2009, pp. 83–86.

Deery, Phillip, 'A Clayton's Cold War', *Overland*, no. 155, 1999.

Deery, Phillip, 'Remembering ASIO', *Overland*, no. 203, Winter 2011.

Dransfield, Michael, *The Second Month of Spring*, ed. Rodney Hall, St Lucia, University of Queensland Press, 1980.

Horner, David, *The Spy Catchers: The Official History of ASIO, 1949–1963*, vol. 1, Allen & Unwin, 2014.

Krygier, Michael, '"Family Intelligence", review of Michael Aarons, *Family File'*, *The Monthly*, July 2010.

Le Carre, John, 'Introduction' to *Tinker, Tailor, Soldier, Spy*, New York, Pocket Books, 2002.

Manne, Robert, *The Petrov Affair*, Melbourne, Text Publishing, 2004.

Mearns, William Hughes, *Antogonish* ('Yesterday upon the stair I met a man who wasn't there...'), 1922.

Montesquieu (Charles Louis de Sevondat, trans.), *The Spirit of Laws (Esprit des lois)*, 1752.

Navasky, Victor, 'Cold War Ghosts', *The Nation*, 28 June 2001.

O'Reardon, Greg, speech at Throssell funeral.

Prichard, Katharine Susannah, *Child of the Hurricane*, Sydney, Angus & Robertson, 1964.

Prichard, Katharine Susannah, *The Real Russia*, Modern Publishers, 1935.

Report of Royal Commission into Espionage. Official transcript of Proceedings, Sydney, 2-18 February 1955.

Throssell, Karen, *The Pursuit of Happiness*, Hyland house, 1988.

Throssell, Ric, *Wild Weeds and Windflowers – the Life and Letters of Katharine Susannah Prichard*, Angus and Robertson, 1975.

Throssell, Ric, *My Father's Son: the last knot untied*, rev. edn., Melbourne, em Press, 1997.

Whitlam, Nicholas & Stubbs, John, *Nest of Traitors*, Brisbane, Jacaranda Press, 1974.

NOTES

p 27. *Canberra Times*, 11 April 1967.

p 27. Andrew Clark, 'Obituary Ric Throssell and Dodie Throssell', *Sydney Morning Herald*, 30 April 1999. Clark was referring to his father, Manning Clark, although he didn't name him.

p 46. Throssell, Ric, *Wild Weeds and Windflowers*, p. 12.

p 48. K.S. Prichard, *Child of the Hurricane*, p 261.

p 71. Throssell, Ric, *My Father's Son*, pp. 369–70.

p 74. *The Petrov Affair*, p. 188. MVD is the Ministry of Internal Affairs (Russia).

p 83. *The Saturday Paper*, 28 April – 4 May 2018.

p 84. Barrister E.F. Hill's address to the Petrov Commission, Printed and Published by R.B. Thompson, 382 King St. Newtown, https://www.reasoninrevolt.net.au/objects/pdf/a000482.pdf.

p 84. W.J. Brown (ed.), *The Petrov Conspiracy Unmasked*, Melbourne, Communist Party of Australia (Marxist-Leninist), 1973, p. 17.

p 86. Richard Pritchard Throssell, Volume 2 Memorandum, 28 May 1954, NAA A6119, 96, folio 45.

p 87. Kislitsyn is also spelled Kislytsin and Kislytson in different sources. Except in direct quotes, Kislitsyn is used throughout this work for the sake of consistency.

p 89. Richard Pritchard Throssell, Volume 2 Memorandum, 21 May 1954, NAA A611957, folio 26.

p 89. Richard Pritchard Throssell, Volume 2 Memorandum, 21 May 1954, NAA A6119 96, folio 28–29.

p 89. Richard Pritchard Throssell , Volume 2 Memorandum, 28 May 1954, NAA A6283.

p 93. R. Manne, *The Petrov Affair*, p. 119.

p 97. R. Throssell, *My Father's Son*, p. 326.

p 99. AA CRS (Bailey papers) M1 509/1 item 35.

p 101. D. Ball and D. Horner, *Breaking the codes*, p.322; Horner, *The Spy Catchers*, p. 298.

p 103. Horner, *The Spy Catchers*, pp. . 367, 353, 298, 368, 358.

p 106. Horner, *The Spy Catchers*, p. 371.

p 106. *Report of Royal Commission on Espionage*, 1955, pp. 141-2.

p 106. Horner, *The Spy Catchers*, p. 369.

p 106. Horner, *The Spy Catchers*, p. 371.

p 107. R. Throssell, *My Father's Son*, p. 319.

p 115. NAA,15 November 1954, A6283, item 20.

p 117. Horner, *The Spy Catchers*, p. 298.

p 119. Quotes from 'Cold War Ghosts', *The Nation*, 28 June 2001.

p 121. P. Deery, 'Remembering ASIO', *Overland* 203, Winter 2011, p. 111.

p 122. R. Throssell, *My Father's Son*, subtitle.

p 157. Charles de Montesquieu, French politician and philosopher (1689-1755).

p 158. M. Carter, *Anthony Blunt – His Lives*, p. 485.

p 158. Attributed to Oliver Cromwell by an anonymous informant quoted in G. Burnet, *History of His Own Time*, 1724.

p 159. E.M. Forster, *What I Believe, and Other Essays*. Freethinker's Classics No. 3, G W Foote. Originally published in *Nation* on July 16, 1938. Quoted by Blunt in 1979: G. Corera, *The Art of Betrayal: Life and Death in the British Secret Service*, Pegasus Books, 2013.

p 160. *Volia*: freedom; lack of restraint or constriction.

p 160-1. Fictional interpretation of information on Vladimir Petrov based on Horner, Whitlam, Manne and Brown.

p 170. Secret letter from Peter Heydon to unknown recipient, dated 24 June 1952, written from the Australian Legation Rio de Janeiro. Quoted in R. Throssell, *My Father's Son*, p. 278.

p 174. Quotes from N. Abjorensen, 'A victim of intelligence game', Canberra Times, 8 October 1996.

p 191. P. Deery, 'Remembering ASIO', p. 111.

p 197. Confidential letter from FH Wheeler, Public Service Board, to Arthur Tange ,14 July 1961, cited in R. Throssell, *My Father's Son*, p. 352. Quotation marks in original.

p 221. M. Krygier, '"Family Intelligence", review of Michael Aarons, *Family File'*, *The Monthly*, July 2010.

p 225. J. Le Carré, 'Introduction' in his *Tinker, Tailor, Soldier, Spy*, New York, Pocket Books, 2002, p. xiii.

p 237. Quotes in this section from P. Deery, 'A Clayton's Cold War?', *Overland*, no. 155, 1999, pp. 89-91.

p 241. Quotes from D. Ball and D. Horner, 'The Moscow Connection', *The Age*. 8 August 1998, p. 111, continued p. 116.

p 245. G. Henderson, 'Cold War secrets and the spies who came out of Canberra', *Sydney Morning Herald*, 12 April 2011.

p 249. D. Ball, 'The spy who came out as Klod', *The Australian*, 24 September 2011.

p 249. D. Ball, 'Soviet spies had protection in very high places', *The Australian*, 14 January 2012.

p 263. ABC Radio National, *Late Night Live*, 24 June 2014. This and other quotes in this section taken from E. Willheim, 'Sex, Spies and Lies? The Spurious Case against John Burton', *Sydney Morning Herald*, 4 Nov 2014.

p 263. Quotes from Pamela Burton in the next two sections refer to her article 'John Burton: Undermined by Dishonest History', *Honest History*, 1 September 2014.

p 267. From Ball's earlier article in *The Australian*, 14 January 2012.

p 298. *Canberra Times*, 11 April 1967.

p 298. D. Batchelor, *The context of Australian playwriting 1939-1968: a case study of the theatre career of Ric Throssell*, Ph. D. diss., University of Queensland, 1995.

IMAGE CREDITS

All photos, paintings, Royal Commission transcripts, unpublished letters to newspapers, family documents (such as postcards) and newspaper cuttings are from the collection of Karen Throssell unless otherwise stated. It has not been possible to identify the actual photographers of the family photos. While every effort has been made to locate the copyright holders of images, the publisher welcomes hearing from anyone in this regard.

Frontispiece: Photo of Ric Throssell 1960s, photographer Gabriel Carpay

p 4: Ric Throssell, Canberra 1996, in front of portrait of Katharine Susannah Pritchard

p 5: Ric Throssell, Dodie Throssell and Dr Louat leaving court in 1955. *Weekend Australian*, 14-15 January 2012

pp 14-15: Family photos. Clockwise from top left: Ric and Dodi, 1980s; Ric and Karen in Canberra, 1957; Hugo, Ric and Katharine, Greenmount, 1924; Ric, 1979; Ric and Karen's daughter Katie, London 1983; painting of Dodie and Karen by Bry Throssell (photo: Janey Stone); Ric, 1976

p 16: *The Australian*, 14 October 1996

p 17: Anonymous retired ASIO officer, *The Australian*, 13 November 2010

p 28: Ric and Katie Throssell (daughter of Karen) reading Shakespeare's *King Lear*, mid 1990s

p 30: Ric as Macbeth

p 39: Katharine Susannah Pritchard, 1945

p 43: Katharine Susannah Pritchard with Karen, 1949

p 53: Katharine Susannah Pritchard in Russia, 1933. Photographer unknown

p 56: Ric and Katharine Susannah Pritchard, 1938

p 63: Karen and daughter Katie ("her Katharine"), Canberra 1987

p 77: Royal Commission on Espionage, *Official transcript of proceedings*, 1 February 1955, front page; 590-631. Ric is sworn in to the hearing

p 85: Vladimir Petrov (centre front) attends the third hearing of Royal Commission on Espionage in Melbourne, 5 July 1954. Photographer unknown

p 87: Vladimir Petrov and Evdokia Petrov inside the safe house in which they were held following their defection to Australia 1954. Photographer unknown

p 88: Royal Commission on Espionage, *Official transcript of proceedings*, 1 February 1955, 499–503

p 95: Royal Commission on Espionage, *Official transcript of proceedings*, 7 February 1955, 597

p 107: Royal Commission on Espionage, *Official transcript of proceedings*, 3 February 1955, 355–356

p 110: *The Age*, 8 August 1998, p 21

p 111: *The Age*, 8 August 1998, p E6

p 128: *The Courier Mail*, 3 October 1996

p 131: Portrait of Dodie Throssell, signed 'Laury', artist not identified. Photo: Janey Stone

p 132: Royal Commission on Espionage, *Official transcript of proceedings*, 4 February 1955, 726–733

p 137: Dorothy Jordan at her graduation ceremony. Photographer unknown

p 140: Diary belonging to Dodie. Photo: Janey Stone

pp 147, 149: Handwritten pages in Dodie's diary. Photos: Janey Stone

p 154: *ASIO Act 1979*, front page. Photo: Janey Stone

p 176: Ric 'arching' Rio de Janeiro, early 1950s

p 183: Karen wearing witches' britches being arrested by plain clothes police, Dean Rusk demonstration January 1966, *Canberra Times*, 28 June 1966, p1

p 188: Royal Commission on Espionage, *Official transcript of proceedings*, 7 February 1955, 702–709

p 195: Ric dressed ready for work, Canberra, 1980s

p 201: Ric at home, Canberra, *Canberra Times*, 5 October 1996

p 212: Royal Commission on Espionage, *Official transcript of proceedings*, 7 February 1955, 710–714

p 242: *The Age*, 22 Apr 1999, p. 2

p 244: Charles Spry, director of ASIO, date unknown, *Weekend Australian*, 13–14 November 2010

p 258: *Weekend Australian*, 14–15 January 2012

p 262: John Burton in 1980s, *Weekend Australian*, 14–15 January 2012

VENONA, ASIO AND COLD WAR ESPIONAGE

PHILLIP DEERY

This essay provides some historical context to a theme that underpins *The Crime of Not Knowing Your Crime*: the basis and truth of the allegation that Ric Throssell was a spy. I will focus on three interrelated aspects: the Venona project; the impact on Throssell of both Venona and the defection of Vladimir and Evdokia Petrov; and the role of ASIO in the early Cold War.

THE COLD WAR BACKDROP

To understand ASIO's role, it's vital to know the context of its establishment in the Cold War atmosphere of Australia from the late 1940s until the mid-1950s. By 1948, international relations had frozen into two competing power blocs. Indeed, the inaugural conference of the Soviet-created Cominform (Communist Information Bureau) in October promulgated a world divided into two intractably hostile camps: a progressive, peace-loving camp led by the Soviet Union and an imperialist, warmongering camp led by the United States. US foreign policy echoed this global division, especially after the 'loss' of China and the loss of her atomic monopoly. Cold War fears and anxieties deepened and intensified. The notion that democracy was under siege from communism was widely held and operated on two levels. The first was the external threat: expansionism from the Soviet Union and the spread of its ideology. The second was the internal fear: subversion from within. The twin questions of national security and loyalty came into sharp focus during the Cold War, and the principal object was the Communist Party.

This intense fear of communism infected domestic politics. During 1949, Lance Sharkey, the general secretary of the Communist Party of Australia (CPA), was jailed for sedition; the defection and 'revelations' of Cecil Sharpley, a former communist leader, led to a lengthy Royal Commission into communism in Victoria; and a bitter general coal strike paralysed the country for two months: union leaders were jailed, Marx House was raided, the Army was deployed as strike-breakers, and the strike was labelled a communist conspiracy. By now, polarisation was complete, and anti-communism was obsessional.

The leading public propagandists and crusaders against communism were the conservative forces in Australian society. In their push to outlaw the CPA, they gained an increasingly sturdy platform, wide audience and more sympathetic reception. The opposition leader, Robert Menzies, promised to ban the CPA if he became prime minister. Implicit in their argument was that legal proscription was necessary only in a state of war. The Party has already been outlawed during a war (by Menzies in 1940) and it now seemed that the only ingredient missing was the sound of the guns. In all other respects, they were engaged in a desperate battle with a dangerous enemy. In June 1950, the guns did sound when the Cold War turned hot in Korea.

As *The Crime of Not Knowing Your Crime* notes in Item #23, when Vladimir and Evdokia Petrov arrived in Canberra from Moscow in February 1951, the political situation in Australia was highly volatile. The newly elected Menzies government had already passed its Communist Party Dissolution Bill. Raids on communists' homes and offices were conducted, printing presses were seized, and plans for internment camps moved from the logistical to the operational. A few weeks after the Petrovs' arrival, the High Court of Australia declared the legislation invalid. Menzies' drive to 'ban the Reds' now moved to the public domain. He announced a referendum to decide the issue: a 'Yes' vote – and this was the position favoured by 70% of Australians at the beginning of the campaign – would give the government the constitutional power to proscribe the CPA. It was a long, gruelling and bitterly fought campaign that deeply gouged the political landscape. Ultimately, the vote was 'No'.

In the middle of the campaign, on 7 July 1951, Petrov met a remarkable, almost bizarre individual at the Russian Social Club. It was Michael Bialoguski, a pro-Soviet, Russian-speaking Polish émigré. Bialoguski was also an ASIO agent. Without him there would have been no defection. And without Petrov's defection there would have been no Royal Commission on Espionage at which he identified Ric Throssell as 'Ferro,' an alleged Soviet spy. This confirmed what the spy catchers apparently already knew, and this knowledge came from Venona.

THE VENONA PROJECT

As *The Crime of Not Knowing Your Crime* has amply demonstrated, it was Venona – the cryptonym used by Western intelligence to denote the remarkable interception and code breaking operation from 1943 to 1980 – that blighted Ric Throssell's life. Non-specific and unanswerable accusations of disloyalty dogged and stymied his career as a diplomat. For 30 years, 'wasted years' Throssell called them, any promotion that required a security clearance was denied. Because Venona was so central to Throssell's life, some background is necessary.

In 1948, the year before ASIO was established, a small group of cryptographers in Washington's Arlington Hall cracked, or decrypted, a portion of previously unbreakable highly classified Soviet diplomatic cables sent between Moscow and its embassies in the Western countries. The top secret Venona project – so secret that it was kept even from President Truman – represented a stunning counterespionage breakthrough. It revealed extensive Soviet espionage networks in the West. The accomplices to this espionage were covert members of communist parties around the world. They achieved, mainly during World War II when the Soviet Union was an ally, high-level penetration of government agencies, bureaucracies and atomic energy establishments. Especially disturbing was the revelation that the US's most closely guarded wartime secret – the Manhattan Project at Los Alamos, which produced the atomic bomb in 1945 – had been penetrated. The decrypted cables were instrumental in identifying key Soviet spies, pointing directly to espionage activity by Klaus Fuchs and Julius Rosenberg and obliquely to Alger Hiss.

Altogether, some 2,900 Soviet intelligence cables were intercepted and, to varying degrees, deciphered. It was not until 1995 that materials from Venona were declassified by the US National Security Agency and details of the project publicly disclosed. The importance of the Venona decrypts to historians of espionage is undeniable. So was their impact at the time: without them, the edifice for McCarthyism would have been more flimsy (J. Edgar Hoover, pivotal to McCarthyism, was privy to Venona); without them, the massive scale of Soviet espionage in the West during the Second World War would have been grossly underestimated; without them, it is improbable that Richard Nixon, spurred on by Hoover, would have been so relentless in his pursuit of Alger Hiss; and without them, ASIO would not have been formed.

It is now indisputable that the establishment of ASIO in March 1949 was due to Venona, not to concerns about the political or industrial strength of the CPA, which by then was declining in influence, prestige and membership. The Venona decrypts revealed that Australia was a poor security risk. This assessment, more than any other factor, prompted a US decision that both shocked and deeply disturbed the Australian government: the abrupt termination of all classified military information flowing from Washington to Canberra. The embargo, on advice from the CIA, recommended by the State-Army-Navy-Air Co-ordinating Committee, and authorised by President Truman, commenced in June 1948 and was not lifted – and then only to a very limited extent – until March 1950. It constituted a serious, if secret, rupture in Australia–US relations; and it automatically downgraded Australia to the lowest category – 'Category E' – among those countries that had diplomatic representation in Washington.

Alarmed by the consequences of this downgrading – the embargo denied access to research data on guided missiles, hindered the development of Australia's defence program and thwarted her aspirations for atomic development – the Chifley government was susceptible to intense British pressure to reorganise its security service. It was British classified information, shared with Australia, that Venona decrypts revealed was passed on to the Soviets. Under the guidance of senior MI5 officials who visited Australia in 1948, a new security service modelled on MI5 structures was created. ASIO was formally established in March 1949, replacing the Commonwealth Investigation Service which transferred its files throughout 1949 and 1950.

The raison d'être of this new organisation was 'The Case': the identification of the nature, extent and source of the leaks of classified information provided by the British, pilfered by Australians and transmitted to the Russians. ASIO, in short, was formed primarily to hunt spies; hence, the title of the first volume of the official history of ASIO.[1] Partially deciphered cables confirmed that the head of Soviet Foreign Intelligence, 'Viktor' (Lieutenant-General Pavel Fitin), had obtained copies of two top-secret documents prepared for the British War Cabinet by the Post-Hostilities Planning Staff. These documents were held by the Department of External Affairs (DEA), in which Ric Throssell worked. The hunt to identify, locate and interrogate those responsible began.

The so-called Australian 'spymaster' identified by Venona was codenamed 'Klod' by the KGB. Klod was Walter Seddon Clayton, a CPA Central Committee member and Control Commission member (responsible for the Party's internal security). Clayton was a shadowy figure. When the Party was outlawed during World War II, it was he who organised the clandestine underground apparatus, and it was he who again prepared the Party for illegality in 1950-51, when the Menzies government sought to ban it first by legislation and then by referendum. ASIO was desperate to uncover both his identity and whereabouts. As Karen Throssell documents in this book, Clayton emerged from hiding to testify at the 1954 Royal Commission on Espionage. He denied all allegations against him, including any contact with Ric Throssell, was not charged and went back into hiding.

Two key members of the Klod group, both in the DEA, were Jim Hill (codenamed 'Tourist') and Ian Milner (codenamed 'Bur'). Hill was a friend of Throssell's and was also the brother of E. F. (Ted) Hill, a prominent communist barrister and secretary of the Victorian branch of the CPA. His role was revealed by a decrypt, which gave the serial number of a DEA diplomatic telegram he, through Clayton, passed to the Soviet Embassy in Canberra. He was interrogated by MI5's legendary William Skardon (who successfully extracted a confession from Klaus Fuchs) but refused to admit to espionage and was never charged. Milner was a New Zealand-born, Oxford-educated diplomat appointed to the Post-Hostilities Division of the DEA in 1944. Throughout 1945 and 1946, he stole and transmitted classified British post-war strategic planning documents, also via Clayton, to the Soviets. After a posting with the UN in New York, Milner relocated permanently – some have said defected – to Prague in 1950, where he was appointed lecturer in English at Charles University and began collaborating with the Czechoslovak security service.[2]

If the Venona decrypted cables are conclusive in the cases of Clayton, Hill and Milner (and others in the DEA), they are, at best, highly circumstantial in the case of Ric Throssell. Venona revealed that Throssell was assigned the codename 'Ferro' by the Soviets. The most incriminating cable, requesting

'Viktor' (Fitin) to ascertain from 'C' (Klod) the following: 'Is it advisable to bring "FERRO" into our work in view of the fact that his mother [Katherine Susannah Prichard] is well known in the Commonwealth [Australia] as an influential ACADEMICIAN?'[3] The only other cable that mentions Throssell by name (he was not then assigned a cover name) was dated 30 September 1945 and concerned a discussion between 'Claude' (Klod) and Prichard about Throssell's diplomatic posting to Moscow. There was no hint by Clayton or his handler, 'Viktor', of recruitment or intelligence exploitation. Instead, the cable reads, 'THROSSEL [sic] is described by "CLAUDE" as a person of limited intelligence. His relations with his mother are normal.'[4] These hardly qualify as valued attributes for espionage activity.

PETROV

ASIO officers interviewed Throssell at length in March 1953 and cleared him: 'We are of the opinion that THROSSELL is a loyal subject and is not a security risk in the Department in which he is employed.'[5] This was despite his refusal to answer questions about his political views, which he considered were 'a purely personal matter', a stand undertaken as a matter of principle – which prompted the unsubstantiated marginal annotation: 'I rather think it was because he had a guilty conscience.' Nevertheless, the two ASIO officers were, in the words of ASIO's Director General, Charles Spry, 'satisfied that he is not, and never has been, a member of the Communist Party or any of its subsidiary organisations, and that he is neither a Communist nor pro-Russian in outlook.' Spry concurred: 'I therefore reduce my assessment of Mr. THROSSELL, and now assess him as not constituting a Security risk to the Commonwealth.'[6]

This changed after the defection of Vladimir and Evdokia Petrov in April 1954. Their statements to ASIO concerning Throssell were both second-hand and sketchy. But in May 1954, he was removed from having access to classified information. Throssell had become a Soviet agent, or so it seemed. What was the evidence? On the day of his defection, Vladimir Petrov told ASIO's Ron Richards:

> Between 1945 and 1948 there was a very serious situation in Australia in the Department of External Affairs. The Communist Party here had a group of External Affairs officers who were giving them official information. The members of the group were transmitting copies of official documents, which they then gave to a Communist Party member. This Party man gave the documents

to Makarov at the Soviet Embassy... I do not know the name of the Party man who at that time reported to Makarov, but his codename was 'Clode' [Klod].[7]

To ASIO, already apprised of Venona, the 'members of the group' included Hill, Milner and Throssell. Vladimir Petrov provided specific information about Throssell. As recounted in *The Crime of Not Knowing Your Crime*, in a statement dated 12 September 1954 and substantially repeated in testimony before the 1954–55 Royal Commission on Espionage (RCE), Petrov wrote:

> I first found out about 'KLODE' from a cable I received from Moscow. In this cable it was indicated to me that THROSSELL's code name was 'FERRO' [and]...that during the war THROSSELL was a member of a group 'KLAUDE' [sic] and that he supplied 'KLAUDE' with very valuable information, not knowing the information he supplied would finally reach the Soviet Embassy.

This was supplemented by Evdokia Petrov's statement to ASIO on 14 September 1954 that she saw a cable – only one – from Moscow about Ferro; it recommended that Philip Kislitsyn, First Secretary at the Embassy and a high ranking KGB officer, discern more about Throssell's 'situation', make an official contact, and await further instructions. Kislitsyn never established contact with Throssell. Evdokia also speculated that Throssell was 'an active agent' who gave the Soviets 'valuable information' when he was posted with his family to Rio de Janeiro.[8]

Meanwhile, Throssell's departmental secretary, Arthur Tange, sought advice from the Solicitor-General, Kenneth Bailey. Although Bailey held the opinion that there were no grounds for charges to be laid against Throssell, he advised Tange in a nine-page legal opinion to use the Public Service Board to transfer Throssell on the basis of the RCE's finding that 'Moscow Centre was interested in Throssell' and wanted him cultivated.[9] Throssell was trapped: he was to be treated, forever, as a 'serious security risk' but was not permitted to discover the reasons why. Only as a last resort, and only if compelled to do so, could he be told that he 'failed to obtain a security clearance' but again requiring no explanation.[10] As this book demonstrates, this Kafkaesque situation, of being found guilty without knowing the charges and without any process of appeal, continued to disfigure Throssell's career as a diplomat and cast a pall over his life. He continued to be 'the man who wasn't there.'[11] Venona and Petrov were his nemeses.

ASIO was effective in neutralising the Klod 'spy ring' (more an informal network of about ten informants than a tight, coherent 'spy ring' in the style of Julius Rosenberg's New York group). No arrests were made – that would have compromised Venona – but ASIO's identification of the group and its espionage activities was directly corroborated by Vladimir Petrov. Thus, one of Petrov's most valued contributions to Western intelligence was his confirmation of Venona's veracity while safeguarding its secrets. What Venona revealed, but could not be disclosed, Petrov affirmed.

So there were spies in Australia, and they did pass secrets. But as we have seen (and this is confirmed by declassified archival files), the case against Throssell was flimsy. It rested primarily on the fact that Throssell was given a cover name by the KGB; that 'Ferro' was mentioned in two decrypted documents; and that he may, unwittingly, have shared information with his communist mother without knowing its ultimate destination, Moscow. The Report of the RCE concluded,

> There are only remote hearsay allegations that, without his knowledge, information said to have come from Throssell reached the Soviet [sic]. There are no particulars of the nature of the information, except that the Moscow Centre regarded it as important or valuable; and there is nothing to show why the Centre so regarded it. There are no particulars as to when it is said to have been given, except that it was during the war. Having regard to the inadequacy of...these indefinite hearsay assertions, and in face of Throssell's denial, it would be wrong to hold that he had been a member of 'Klod's Group' or that he had wittingly given any information.[12]

In short, then, the RCE exonerated Throssell. That leaves Venona. It must be remembered that, although some Venona intercepts were conclusive, others must be treated with caution and circumspection. Venona is fragmentary, raw and 'one-way' intelligence data. The cable-senders could exaggerate, and the cable-breakers could misinterpret. And until the relevant Soviet archives are fully opened, we will not know what the cable-receivers in Moscow believed. Yet none of this deterred a senior MI5 officer from concluding that 'there can be no reasonable doubt that Throssell was at one time an active and conscious spy',[13] or a senior Foreign Office official, commenting on the RCE, that 'It may be taken as certain that THROSSELL and HILL were guilty of espionage', that Throssell had 'taken fright during his service in Rio de Janeiro', and that this was 'likely' to have been 'occasioned by HILL's interrogation.'[14] These judgements were shared with and by Spry.

There were wider security implications to ASIO's connecting Throssell with espionage. ASIO made little meaningful distinction between the small handful of 'non-legal' or covert communists who undoubtedly engaged in espionage activities (such as Wally Clayton, Jim Hill or Ian Milner) and the thousands of CPA members and 'fellow travellers' who immersed themselves in daily struggles within trade unions, on local councils and through 'front' organisations; who campaigned for better working conditions and greater social justice; who sided with the underprivileged and the dispossessed; and who were neither aware of espionage nor would have sanctioned it. Of the 23,000 Australian communists in 1944 (its peak, when espionage did occur), about 22,990 were not involved in passing classified information to the Soviet Union. But both groups have been tarred with the same brush of disloyalty and treason. In ASIO's world view in the 1950s and 1960s, communism, subversion and spying (or the potential for spying) became synonymous. The categories were interchangeable, and this haunted both communists and those lawfully supporting the communist ideology during the early Cold War.

BEYOND ESPIONAGE?

ASIO's counterespionage brief – its unremitting pursuit of 'The Case', which was triggered by Venona, assisted by the Petrovs' defections and claimed Throssell as a casualty – was increasingly supplemented by its counter-subversion function. Here, ASIO crossed the Rubicon from being a professional agency that collected, evaluated and transmitted intelligence, to a sometimes disreputable, often politicised and always shadowy presence, not monitoring only communists but also peace activists, scientists, academics, writers and, surprisingly, even judges,[15] many of whom were not members of the CPA. It is difficult to discern how these individuals were 'working towards the forcible overthrow of constitutional government' – Justice Hope's definition of subversion during the first Royal Commission on Intelligence and Security (1974–77). The human costs of ASIO's monitoring of domestic dissenters are difficult to measure. It is only through finely grained research that the historian can reveal otherwise hidden stories of personal damage inflicted by ASIO on lawful protesters alleged to be subversives. Some of my own research has uncovered several such stories.[16]

In these, and in a great many other cases, we can observe how lives were altered and careers obstructed by ASIO. When individuals engaged in lawful political dissent, they were 'adversely recorded' or considered subversive. The word 'subversive' was crucial. Protection of the nation against subversion was one of ASIO's principal functions, yet it was a vague and slippery concept. Neither the prime ministerial executive order that established ASIO in 1949 nor the *Australian Security Intelligence Organization Act 1956* provided any definition of subversion. As Mr Justice Hope commented in 1977, this opened the door to the Organisation and its officers 'mistaking mere dissent or non-conformity for subversion' and thereby impinging on 'legitimate political behaviour.'[17] Very few of ASIO's left-wing targets constituted a sufficient threat to national security to justify ASIO's compilation of dossiers, reliance on informants, vetting for public service boards, and immigration and passport controls. The individual cases are a tiny part of a much bigger story of harassment in the early Cold War. Organisations that had a pronounced left-wing bias – particular trade unions, community associations, university groups, Labor Party branches – were also targeted and subjected to politicised surveillance.

Assessing this period, the Hope Royal Commission on Intelligence and Security concluded that 'until quite recently, ASIO could not be taken seriously as an efficient organisation, still less an effective security organisation.' In his report, Hope noted an 'insufficient understanding [within ASIO] of ASIO's goals and purposes'; he also noted ASIO's 'poor leadership' and 'very bad personnel management practices', including 'inadequate training, lack of professional standards, etc.' These flaws shaped its intelligence assessment: in this area, Hope wrote, 'I saw little evidence in ASIO that the qualities of mind and expertise needed were recognized, or available in any large measure.'[18] Spry himself was concerned about such deficiencies. At a meeting with two senior ASIO officers in 1973, after noting that many ASIO officers were 'unsuitable' for the positions they held:

> He considered that the standard of professionalism within the organisation was very poor and didn't feel that he could rely upon much of the advice he received.[19]

This history of unethical, unprofessional or flawed behaviour is in danger of being forgotten. In the post-9/11 era, when counterterrorism took precedence over its counterespionage and counter-subversion priorities, ASIO has acquired a higher degree of political respectability and moral legitimacy. Since 2001, its staff numbers have trebled, its budget has grown by 535 percent to $1.4 billion per annum and, according to Hocking, its powers have expanded to such an extent that civil liberties are imperilled.[20] In May 2020, then Minister for Home Affairs, Peter Dutton, introduced the Australian Security Intelligence Organisation Bill 2020, which contains even more sweeping and draconian provisions.[21] Its massive new Canberra headquarters, officially the Ben Chifley Building but nicknamed Lubyanka by the Lake, occupies the size of three city blocks, opened to staff in 2015, and cost $680 million.

ASIO's tawdry past – its improprieties, its smearing, its often-dubious intelligence acquired from even more dubious informants and its occasional unlawful actions – have all been sidestepped as the reputation of this, the most critical of Australia's six intelligence agencies, is rehabilitated and transformed. But the early history of ASIO's defective and partisan behaviour in the Cold War years should not be forgotten. If, as Milan Kundera once wrote, 'The struggle of man against power is the struggle of memory against forgetting', then this book, *The Crime of Not Knowing Your Crime*, provides us with compelling reasons to remember the case of Ric Prichard Throssell.

FURTHER READING

Burgmann, Meredith, *Dirty Secrets: Our ASIO Files*, Sydney, NewSouth, 2014.

Capp, Fiona, *Writers Defiled: Security Surveillance of Australian Authors and Intellectuals 1920–1960*, Melbourne, McPhee Gribble, 1993.

Curthoys, Ann and Damousi, Joy (eds.), W*hat did you do in the Cold War, Daddy? Personal Stories From a Troubled Time*, Sydney, NewSouth, 2014.

Hutchinson, Kate, *Extreme and Dangerous: The Curious Case of Dr Ian Macdonald*, Melbourne, Australian Scholarly Publishing, 2020.

Keenan, Haydn (dir.), *Persons of Interest*, 2004. https://www.smartstreetfilms.com.au/catalogue/persons-of-interest-dvd.

Throssell, Ric, *My Father's Son*, Melbourne, William Heinemann, 1989.

ENDNOTES
Venona, ASIO and Cold War espionage

1. D. Horner, *The Spy Catchers: The Official History of ASIO, 1949–1963*, vol. 1, Allen & Unwin, 2014.

2. See P. Deery, 'Cold War Victim or Rhodes Scholar Spy? Revisiting the case of Ian Milner', *Overland*, no. 147, 1997.

3. Cable, Moscow to Canberra, '"C" [Klod] to Report on Various Agents (1948)', 5 June 1948. 'Academician' was probably code for CPA member.

4. Cable, Canberra to Moscow, '"CLAUDE" Reports on Throssell (1945)', 30 September 1945.

5. NAA: A6119, 95.

6. C.C.F. Spry to R.G. Casey, 1 April 1953, NAA: A6119, 95.

7. *Report of the Royal Commission on Espionage*, 1955, para 405, pp. 119-20.

8. NAA: A6119, 96; NAA: A6283, 79. On 'The Case Concerning Throssell', see Ball and Horner, *Breaking the Codes*, pp. 321-5.

9. Bailey to Tange, 22 October 1955, NAA: M1505, 1287.

10. Spry to John Crawford (Secretary to the Department of Commerce and Agriculture), 18 May 1955, NAA: A1509, 35.

11. R. Throssell, *My Father's Son*, Melbourne, William Heinemann, 1989, p. 400. His repeated attempts to discover the reason(s) he was denied a full security clearance and, thus, promotion, continued until December 1987, when the Administrative Appeals Tribunal determined that the disclosure of 10 documents critical to his case was 'contrary to the public interest' and 'could cause damage to the security of the Commonwealth'. It further determined that 'disclosure of any of the documents would reveal, or assist in revealing, the source from which certain information concerning the applicant was communicated, on an understanding of strict confidentiality, to [ASIO].' Probably, the 'source' referred to was Venona, which in 1987 was still a tightly guarded secret. See http://www7.austlii.edu.au/cgi-bin/viewdoc/au/cases/cth/AATA/1987/454.html.

12. *Report of the Royal Commission on Espionage*, 1955, para 505, pp. 141-2.

13. Memorandum, 13 October 1955, para 11, 'Vladimir Mikhailovich PETROV/Evdokia Alexeyevna PETROVA: Russian', The National Archives, Great Britain (TNA): KV 2/3451, folio 575a. An accompanying Minute Sheet (C.P.C. de Wesselow to D.I.A., 13 October 1955) recorded Throssell as 'Probably conscious agent... Under study for reactivation.'

14. Letter, 'Top Secret and Personal', G.R. Mitchell to A J. de la Mare, 15 April 1955, TNA: KV2/3449.

15. See M. Finnane, *JV Barry: A Life*, Sydney, UNSW Press, 2007.

16. See, for example, '"Dear Mr. Brown": Migrants, security and the Cold War', *History Australia*, vol. 2, no. 2, 2005, pp. 40-52; 'Scientific freedom and post-war politics: Australia, 1945-1955', *Historical Records of Australian Science*, vol. 13, no. 1, 2000, pp. 1-19; 'Science, security and the Cold War: An Australian dimension', *War and Society*, vol. 17, no. 1, 1999, pp. 81-99; '"A dangerous trend towards authoritarianism": Dr James, the Menzies government and Cold War Australia', in P. Griffiths and R. Webb (eds,), *Work, Organisation, Struggle*, Canberra, Australian Society for the Study of Labour History, 2001, pp. 120-6.

17. *Royal Commission on Intelligence and Security: Fourth Report*, Volume I, 34-55 (on 'Subversion'), NAA: A8908, 4A.

18. *Supplement to Fourth Report*, Copy no. 2, 3-4; *Fourth Report*, Volume I, 675. On the damning *Fourth Report*, see Peter Edwards, *Law, Politics and Intelligence: A Life of Robert Hope*, Sydney, New South, 2020, pp. 183-9.

19. 'Notes on Discussion with the Director General on 21 September 1973', 4, 3 October 1973, NAA: A12385, AI/37.

20. Jenny Hocking, *Terror Laws: ASIO, Counter-Terrorism and the Threat to Democracy*, Sydney, UNSW Press, 2003, chapters 12-13.

21. Greg Barns, 'ASIO changes are step towards totalitarian state', *The Age*, 14 May 2020, p. 18.

Red Swan Series

WESTERN AUSTRALIAN RADICAL LABOUR HISTORY AND POLITICS

The Red Swan series in radical Western Australian Labour history and politics, published by interventions, brings to life stories from the workers' movement and social movements that need to be told. It offers a perspective on the state's history and politics that challenges the status quo.

Red Swan Series

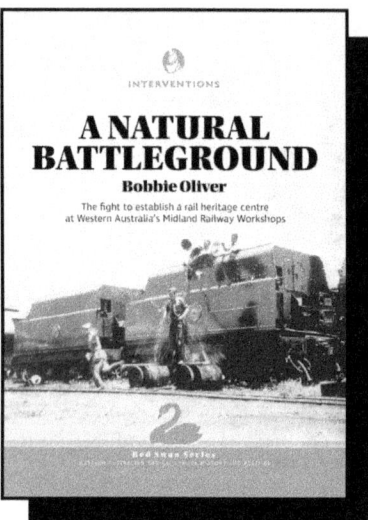

'Often those in power would prefer us to forget yesteryear's struggles, the easier to mould tomorrow to their interests. Bobbie Oliver brilliantly illuminates why we must not forget the Midland Railway Workshops – and so lights a way forward for Western Australia and other challenging sites around the post-industrial world.'

Colin Divall Emeritus Professor of Railway Studies
University of York, UK

A Natural Battleground:
The fight to establish a rail heritage centre at
Western Australia's Midland Railway Workshops
Bobbie Oliver
Red Swan Series 1
2019

When the Government Railway Workshops at Midland closed on 4 March 1994, Western Australia lost a major trainer and employer of skilled tradespeople and much of its heavy industry. Former workers feared that their history of industrial achievements on the factory floor and through union action would also be lost. Despite expending considerable resources and promising to honour a "proud history" and create an "exciting future", the development authorities have done little to redevelop the site. A Natural Battleground is the story of the fight to save the buildings from demolition and dedicate space in them for a rail heritage centre to preserve the Workshops' history. The first aim was achieved, the second is merely a hope. As the author says, "Somewhere in these buildings, decency dictates, there must be space to tell the whole story of what happened here, including what happened to those workers whose lives were irrevocably changed by their closure."

Whether you are interested in the history of trade unions, heritage or railways this book will engage and inspire you.

Red Swan Series

Radical Perth, Militant Fremantle
Edited by Charlie Fox, Alexis Vassiley,
Bobbie Oliver and Lenore Layman
Interventions 2020

This book tells 34 fascinating stories of radical moments In the cities' past, from as long ago as the 1890s and as recent as Occupy. The revised 2nd edition brings four new tales including the unknown story of striking Chinese seamen on the Fremantle waterfront, who faced brutal repression, but won support from Fremantle unionists. It also includes student radicalism at Curtin University (then WAIT), Perth's very-own Green Bans and solidarity with the famous strike of Aboriginal pastoral workers.

It also includes the 1998 Maritime Union of Australia dispute on Fremantle's waterfront, the revolutionary theatre of the Workers Art Guild; a riot of unemployed workers outside the Treasury building; rock concerts inside St Georges Cathedral; bodgies and widgies cutting up the dance floor at the Scarborough Beach Snake Pit; the Point Peron women's peace camp, and much more.

www.ingramcontent.com/pod-product-compliance
Lightning Source LLC
Chambersburg PA
CBHW070713020526
44107CB00078B/2371